Small Cogs in a Large Wheel

Naresh Nandan Prasad

Small Cogs in a Large Wheel

A Civil Servant's Life

WESTLAND
NON-FICTION

First published by Westland Non-Fiction, an imprint of Westland Books, a division of Nasadiya Technologies Private Limited, in 2023

No. 269/2B, First Floor, 'Irai Arul', Vimalraj Street, Nethaji Nagar, Alapakkam Main Road, Maduravoyal, Chennai 600095

ISBN: 9789357768320

10 9 8 7 6 5 4 3 2 1

The views and opinions expressed in this work are the author's own and the facts are as reported by him, and the publisher is in no way liable for the same.

The quotes from personal conversations may not be verbatim, as they are based on the author's memory.

Typeset by SÜRYA, New Delhi

Printed at Parksons Graphics Pvt. Ltd

CONTENTS

FOREWORD

Few persons have had the depth of experience as a civil servant that Naresh Prasad had. He worked at all levels of government, starting, as is customary in the Indian Administrative Service, at the district and state levels, moving to the national level and then concluding his long and distinguished career at the international level as the chief of staff and assistant director general of the World Intellectual Property Organization (WIPO) in Geneva, Switzerland. It was in this last capacity that I came to know, work with and admire Naresh during my two terms as director general of WIPO.

A civil servant, especially one in the upper echelons of the service, is in a privileged position to witness the main developments, trends and dramas that occur in public life. Bearing witness is what this memoir is all about. They tell the human side of public service: the camaraderie of colleagues; the development of friendships; the balance of public service, which may lead to postings far from home and family life; the relationship with superiors, often holding political positions; the maintenance of integrity in the face of all sorts of challenges; and openness to new experiences and new people from all walks of life. In this respect, this memoir provides a blueprint for what someone contemplating public service might expect and is an invaluable guide to aspirants to public service.

Over the twelve years during which I had the privilege of working with Naresh Prasad, several characteristics of his stood out and impressed me deeply. One was his profound commitment to integrity, in all its respects—the integrity of decisions from unwarranted political interference, the integrity of the process leading to decisions and the protection of the independence of that process, and scrupulous honesty in relation to the use and deployment of the employing entity's financial and human resources. Naresh was a model of the highest standards that we may justifiably expect from those who decide to devote their professional lives to the service of the public.

How does one manage to maintain integrity so successfully? The memoir provides a hint of the key to success: '... if civil servants do not get too attached to their positions and places of posting, they can work in an upright and fearless manner. It is only when civil servants seek favours from their political masters that they have to go down the path of subservience and even cowardice.'

In other words, avoid conflicts of interest, where a personal interest may cause you to compromise a professional duty.

Equally impressive was the fierce loyalty that Naresh

practised in relation to those who worked immediately for him or for whom he worked, as well as his loyalty to his employing entity and its mission. While perhaps, in many respects, an old-fashioned virtue in an age of often unseemly attempts to be in the limelight of the myriad forms of media, loyalty to one's colleagues and employer returns rich dividends and creates a sure foundation for professional relationships. Naresh was a deeply loyal colleague, friend and human being.

It goes without saying that a person does not rise in the civil service, whether national or international, without being competent. Naresh was an excellent manager of people and knew how to mobilise resources in order to achieve the desired result, with a very pragmatic and no-nonsense approach. During our time together at WIPO, a massive programme of change was undertaken, affecting all parts of the organisation and its culture and services. Naresh was an important part of this organisation-wide effort, participating with his characteristic calmness and capacity to place everything in its proper context.

Naresh Prasad was also an astute observer of political behaviour and trends at all levels, from staff politics to departmental politics, to national and, ultimately, international politics. His insights were always interesting and he was able to use this talent in fashioning appropriate policies in the execution of his multiple mandates. He was also able to converse on politics in an interesting and dispassionate manner, largely leaving judgements to be formed by the other participants in the conversation, rather than imposing rigid views upon them.

We shall all miss Naresh immensely. His passing was extremely untimely, depriving him and his family of a well-earned gentler and more relaxed participation in life than full-time duties permit. He has left us with rich memories and, now, this fine memoir that brings to life so many of those memories.

Dr Francis Gurry

Dr Francis Gurry is an Australian national who, from 2008 to 2020, was the fourth director general of the World Intellectual Property Organization. During that time, he was also secretary-general of the International Union for the Protection of New Varieties of Plants. Dr Gurry is a world-renowned figure in the field of intellectual property.

CHAPTER ONE

NOMINATION

In January 2019, the permanent representative of India to the United Nations met the permanent secretary of the Department of Industrial Property and Promotion, the nodal department of the Government of India, for matters concerning the World Intellectual Property Organization (WIPO), a Geneva-based specialised agency of the United Nations that deals with matters of innovation and creativity. He proposed that it would be worth considering my nomination for the post of director general (DG) of WIPO, a post which would fall vacant in 2020 after the completion of a two-term tenure by the incumbent DG, Francis Gurry. The Permanent Secretary wholeheartedly endorsed the proposal.

In the last week of June 2019, I learnt from authoritative sources in the office of the minister for Commerce and Industry that the minister, Piyush Goyal, had approved my nomination and the proposal was being sent to the Ministry of External Affairs.

In July 2019, Gurry called on Goyal. The meeting took place in the latter's office. I was present at that meeting. The DG conveyed his decision not to seek re-election.

At the launch event of the Global Innovation Index, published by WIPO, the minister for Commerce and Industry told both the DG and me that he would request the minister for External Affairs, S. Jaishankar, to issue instructions to the Indian missions abroad to 'lobby' for my candidature with key countries.

Between June and December 2019, the permanent representative and ambassador of India sent several messages to New Delhi strongly endorsing my candidature. Some messages even concluded that if I was a candidate, India could be assured of an easy win; I would be the first Indian as the head of an agency in the past six decades. Several key ambassadors in Geneva also conveyed their strong support for my candidature.

In mid-September 2019, I was informed that the foreign secretary had cleared the proposal for my nomination and sent it to Jaishankar.

Everything fell silent after that, giving rise to a lot of rumours and speculation. With such a massive and strong endorsement at all levels, why was India not pushing ahead with its candidature?

Several theories were doing the rounds. Was it a matter of geopolitical considerations? Was WIPO not an important enough agency to merit consideration? Was it a simple case of personal vendetta? Or was it the famous rivalry between the

Indian Administrative Service (IAS) and the Indian Foreign Service? It could also be petty jealousies at play. The silence was baffling.

The last date for the nomination, 30 December 2019, came and went. Yet, there was no word from Delhi. It got curiouser and curiouser. Geneva-based diplomats could not conceal their surprise. A lot of that was directed towards me. But I had no answer.

Indian officials visiting Geneva made stray, callous and irresponsible statements, adding fuel to fire. The Indian candidature, or the lack of it, became the talk of the town—or rather this 'big village', as I have often referred Geneva to be. Plenty of malicious gossip crept in, and I was the centre of that gossip. I decided to keep my lips sealed in the hope that one day the truth would be out. What exactly happened in the office of India's Foreign Minister who I had never met or seen?

After a hiatus of more than six months, on 22 July 2020, the United States secretary of state, Mike Pompeo, while addressing the US–India Business Council at the India Ideas Summit, stated that the US welcomed India's partnership in multilateral diplomacy. He went on to praise India's work together with the US on the WIPO election. Pompeo said, 'Together our countries ensured that the new Director General of the Organization would respect Intellectual Property Rights and the US welcomed the election of Daren Tang from Singapore to the post.'

At last, some clarity was emerging, but to my mind that is not the full truth. It was an excellent cover-up and a ploy to block my nomination. As our motto 'Satyamev Jayate' says, the truth shall always prevail. It will all come out one day is my firm conviction. Remember, one can fool some people all the time, all people sometimes, but not all the people all the time.

Forty years of my career in the Indian Civil Service are best captured by this episode. That is why I have given it the primacy it deserves. Read on to know more about the Civil Service.

Each of the statements made above is verifiable in official files and documents. I have refrained from disclosing the identity of my sources to protect them from backlash and vindictive action. It may be good for people to remember that having been a part of the Civil Service for decades, I do enjoy the friendship and support of several colleagues. And they have been my constant companions in this maze that makes the Indian Civil Service.

CHAPTER TWO

THE JOURNEY BEGINS

Monday, 31 August 1981. An important day in my life. It was the day I left my parents' home in New Delhi to take my first steps into a world without safety nets. I set off for Old Delhi Railway Station, India's oldest and busiest train station. I had with me a big black trunk containing my life's belongings—at twenty-four, that basically meant a few slacks, some shirts and socks—to start what would become an unforgettable journey into the unknown. I was leaving the security of my parents' home, the doting affection of a caring mother, a protective father who shielded me from the hardships of making my own decisions, loving siblings and a social circle that provided comfort for the shy, quiet young man I was at the time.

I reached the train station in time for the 10 p.m. Mussoorie Express, headed to the remote town of Dehradun, the rail head for Mussoorie, Uttarakhand (then a part of Uttar Pradesh), a quaint hill station developed by the British for their summer sojourns in the foothills of the Himalayas. Mussoorie was home to the Lal Bahadur Shastri National Academy of Administration (LBSNAA), a research and training institute on public policy and public administration. Operated by the union government, its main purpose is to train Civil Service officers belonging to the IAS.

As I bid a teary farewell to my parents, little did I realise that on the same train was the person who would become my life partner. While I was sad to leave home, I felt that the contours of a magnificent adventure were being drawn. My greatest ambition was to have a loving family of my own, modelled on the home environment that I had just left behind. That is not to say that I did not have any professional ambitions. But a closely knit family and good, lifelong friends topped the list. On that train, I also met men and women who have remained close friends since that day in August 1981.

At the time, seated in a second-class, air-conditioned coach on the train, we were all strangers but with similar professional ambitions. It was a huge honour to be accepted to LBSNAA. Along with that, we all had a strong sense of pride in common. After all, we belonged to the coveted group of the top hundred out of a quarter million aspirants, having cleared one of the stiffest recruitment processes in India. We also shared a range of mixed feelings—joy, anticipation, homesickness—all bottled up as we embarked on a new path. We started chatting with one another without knowing names or backgrounds. Our strongest bond at that time was our common destination.

The train pulled into Dehradun, then a quiet, sleepy town, but there was nevertheless something in the air that left me mystified. If I had known that this would become a city I would have so many connections with, I would have taken more time to breathe in the clear, fresh air, and appreciate my first steps in the journey that would become the rest of my life. Many of the people that mean the most to me today stepped off that train with me: my future wife, my future best friends. This town gave me some of my closest relationships, both personal and professional, including one who had not yet stepped into this world!

We boarded the buses that took us to the academy. And this is where my first encounter with bureaucracy began. For almost two hours, we were locked in the painful process of registration. My only concern at the time was to call home and reassure my parents that I had arrived safely. But this was the 1980s. There were no mobile phones—smart or otherwise—no SMSes and no social media. I could not conveniently tweet a photo of the superb landscape standing majestically before me or check-in on Facebook. In fact, the only long-distance phone connection we could get was a three-kilometre walk from the academy at the post office at Library Point. The phone call had to wait.

As we completed the formalities, we were each allotted our rooms. I was assigned to the Kaveri block and shared a room with someone who became one of my best and most loyal friends. We were generously given half a day to settle in until dinner, our first brush with some of the most inedible food that would be served to us for months to come, a true hallmark of the academy mess. How I missed my mother's cooking! We ate, we mingled and enjoyed the crisp weather of the evening.

The next morning, we were asked to convene in the forecourt of the academy for a physical training class which included a four-kilometre jog. I was not much of a jogger but I arrived in my running attire ready to impress. Within minutes of my arrival, I was distracted by a woman who fully fit into my concept of an Indian beauty. She stole my heart in seconds. She had long silky hair, cascading well below her knees, and piercing eyes that spoke a thousand words. Her look reflected authenticity and strength but also warmth. I took a step forward and looked sideways. I had to find out more about this woman. Little did I know at the time that I was looking at my life partner.

CHAPTER THREE

THE FOUNDATION COURSE

The foundation course is a rite of passage for officer trainees of the All-India Services: the IAS, the Indian Police Service (IPS), the Indian Forest Service, the Indian Foreign Service and various central services.

The course kicked off on 1 September 1981 and went on up to 30 November 1981. They were the most challenging and the most fun three months of my life. The course groups fresh entrants to the academy and aims to familiarise them with a range of issues: political, social, economic and administrative. The academy website says this course equips officers 'with requisite skills, knowledge and attitudes to shoulder the responsibilities of a public service officer'. More interestingly though is the part that says: 'The Academy stands out as one of the very few institutions in the world with focus not only on Civil Service capacity building but also inter-services camaraderie and cooperation.' I liked the emphasis on 'camaraderie'.

I created some of the strongest bonds of my life during that short period of three months. The website description is spot-on. But let me share what the website does not tell you.

The course brought together about 500 wide-eyed, ambitious, curious young men and women. Very quickly, small groups—not to say cliques—began to emerge. I naturally gravitated towards my train companion. As fate would have it, he also became my roommate and partner in mischief at the academy. Over the next fortnight, we were joined by three other male colleagues—one from the Foreign Service and two from the Police Service—and two women colleagues, one from the Postal Service and the other from the Railways. It was a formidable combination. The seven of us (Partha, Rakesh Maria, Manoj Bhatt, Devika, Anjali, Anil and I) became inseparable, spending all our non-working, non-sleeping hours together. I was nicknamed 'Nainoo', a name that stayed with me despite my strong reservations.

A typical day began with physical training, followed by a hefty jog to help us build an appetite for a hearty yet quick breakfast. A series of dreary classes on subjects ranging from Indian history to constitutional law to economics ensued. Little did our teachers know that most of the students were totally distracted and hardly paid attention to the lectures. I used a big chunk of the time to write to my family and friends back home. The relationship with my family was changing, possibly maturing, but I digress.

Classes would finish at around 4 p.m. Having eaten some thoroughly inedible food for lunch, we would look forward to the evening to find something more appetising. The seven of us would get together after class and stroll down to the corner shop just outside the academy, in the crisp September weather, to gorge on some snacks. We would then return to the academy and gulp down our dinner. And then our night would begin in earnest.

We strolled the roads and alleys, treating ourselves to some paan and, on occasion, Cadbury's chocolate (at the time a bar cost 25 paise). As the night grew colder, we would huddle in some hidden corner of the academy, covered in shawls and blankets, talking, joking and singing for hours. Two people in our group were very talented singers. Those times were unforgettable.

However, the academy was not all bad food and dreary classes interspersed with stolen moments with friends. It was also a fun experience. I would like to think that I contributed to the fun. We started the tradition of cultural evenings. Partha became the culture secretary, with Anil and I chipping in towards organising the first event. This was a time-consuming activity, involving coordination, casting and, at times, having to cajole colleagues out of their shells. Among the many musical performances, one song remains etched in my memory till today. It was a Haryanvi song in which Anjali and I participated. Given the success of the first cultural event, they soon became a regular feature of the academy.

I took over from Partha as the culture secretary and was tasked with organising a cultural evening in the rather depressing days that followed the foundation course. The obvious choice was a skit on the management of the academy. Our course director, Sunder Burra, who had a very distinctive and laboured style of speaking, gave me lots of material which I turned into my first attempt at stand-up comedy. It was the first time I realised I had a special talent of mimicking people. Hearing an entire hall bursting with laughter was all the acknowledgement that I needed to continue developing this skill. And Mr Burra was pleased—after all, imitation is the highest form of flattery.

Another highlight of this course was a Himalayan trek. We were organised into small groups. I chose the Kedarnath-Badrinath trek. Badrinath and Kedarnath are two of the holiest shrines for Hindus, dedicated to lords Vishnu and Shiva. The trek was fascinating—it not only tested our physical strength but also our mental resilience and patience. We were groups of about thirty, travelling in one bus, at times sharing the same room and, much to the chagrin of many, with very limited toilet facilities.

The most difficult trek was an uphill thirteen-kilometre walk on very difficult terrain under pouring rain from Govindghat to Ghangaria, en route to Hemkund Sahib, considered to be one of the holiest pilgrimages for the Sikh community, and the Valley of Flowers, a UNESCO world heritage site. When we finally reached our destination, the sight of a vendor making hot parathas with a single cube of butter on each was heavenly. By the time our trek ended, layers of fatigue had kicked in and I recall gobbling down more than a dozen omelette parathas. After that hearty meal, about twenty of us huddled into one room while five girls settled down in an adjacent one.

One of the female probationers was an urbane, attractive, well-educated graduate from one of Delhi's top-notch colleges. Being fussy about clean, comfortable toilets was par for the course. The surroundings did not match her expectations. Especially since the only toilet in the ladies' room seemed endlessly occupied. That is when our friend came running into our room screeching, 'Naresh, Naresh, where is the loo?' As soon as she said this, one of my colleagues who was unaware that, apart from referring to hot winds that blow in the plains during summers, 'loo' also meant toilet, said, 'Naresh, *itthe toh burf padh rahi hai par ye kudi loo, loo, loo kyon kitti hai'* (It's freezing cold here but why is this woman saying loo, loo, loo?). Everyone burst out laughing. This could not but earn her the nickname of 'Loo' which, for better or for worse, she has kept till today. At one point, she suspected that I was behind the label but I feigned ignorance. Little did I know then that she would later become my future wife's roommate at the Railway Academy in Baroda and that we would go on to become very good friends.

Another mandatory part of the foundation course was a week-long village attachment. I was part of a group that went to a remote village located in the faraway district of Hardoi, Uttar Pradesh. The village had no electricity or running water, and we slept on matted cots in the open air. The only memorable occurrence from that attachment was a brush with a huge—not to mention very scary—king cobra. As I opened the window of the dilapidated Public Works Department guest house—fortunately on a moonlit night—where we were housed, I sensed something rise. It was the hood of a mighty snake that was about to sting my hand. A king cobra's bite releases neurotoxic venom that disrupts communication between nerve cells, bringing about paralysis of muscles around the lungs and disturbing the cardiac rhythm. In layperson's terms, the bite kills you. Very instinctively, I withdrew a few steps even as I was hypnotised. Fortunately, the snake decided to spare me and slid away from the window sill, down the wall into the green patch of land around the guest house. And I lived to tell the tale.

I would be remiss if I didn't say a word about my finances during my months at the academy. We were given a paltry salary of seven hundred rupees a month, of which four hundred and fifty rupees went to the academy. That left us with two hundred and fifty rupees to 'splurge'. Believe it or not, we lived like kings. We had enough for our daily dose of chocolates, paan, snacks and a couple of trips to Delhi (the bus fare was fifteen rupees one way). Amazingly, we never fell short of money. That is something that I have maintained all my life—be content and satisfied with what you have and make the best of every situation. Happiness is not measured by the amount of money you have but the moments that make you happy. Some of my happiest days were spent at the academy.

The days raced by and suddenly it was 30 November 1981. The probationers from the other services had to leave. Those in the IAS would stay on for their professional course. I suddenly realised that five of my closest friends from our gang of seven were to leave. At the farewell dinner that night, we were confronted by the harsh reality that we could be meeting for the last time as a group. We had mixed feelings—mostly sad that we were separating, but also happy and comforted by the belief that the bonds we had created over the past three months would last forever. Unfortunately for my budding love, Anjali too had to leave for her training at the Railway Staff College (RSC) at Baroda. We had not said a word about our feelings for each other.

Having kept an eye on the evolution of the academy over the years, I am pleased to see that it is no longer desperate—like it was during my years there—to convert young people into British-style civil servants. The focus now is on India's culture and ethnicity, of which we are so proud. During my time, we had sit-down dinners with signs saying, 'Men in ties only'. We had wanted to put that to the literal test at one point—and were lectured on table etiquette.

CHAPTER FOUR

THE PROFESSIONAL COURSE

Soon after completing the foundation course, IAS officers graduate to Phase I training. Starting in December, it runs up to May of the following year and comprises academic instruction and a winter study tour. The winter study tour, Bharat Darshan, includes a fascinating tour of India, or rather a part of India. This is followed by a year of district training in the officer's allotted state cadres. A so-called Phase II, a six-week course at the LBSNAA, rounds up the training.

Bharat Darshan was a phenomenal experience. I was part of a group of twenty-five all-male probationers, a rather feisty and boisterous group to say the least. We even earned the nickname 'rowdies'. The group leader was my roommate. His task was to be an arduous one.

My Bharat Darshan spanned almost a month. It took me to historical and fascinating towns, cities and reserve forests. The tour also included attachments in a tribal village, with a cooperative federation, a public sector undertaking. Finally, we were lucky to partake in a stint with the Parliament in New Delhi.

The Bharat Darshan experience was indeed memorable and included several interesting moments. On New Year's Eve of 1981, we were in Mandla District in the state of Madhya Pradesh, a predominantly tribal district. We arrived late in the evening and the first thing the 'rowdies' did was to go looking for a liquor shop. How else could we live up to our reputation! Much to our disappointment, all we could find was lots of country-made liquor. But we were all optimists—the glass was always half full (especially when it came to liquor!)—so we saw the bright side: the 'efficacy' of this liquor was much higher than the usual brands.

The next challenge was to find enough goat meat to cook a nice mutton curry for dinner. Three of my colleagues volunteered to do the cooking in the open air despite the chill of a winter night. Inside, the latest Hindi film songs—generally dance and cabaret numbers—were resonating loudly. The scene was set for an all-round great New Year's party. Yet, the group leader was sweating.

Amid this chaos, a staff representative from the academy, Muthusamy, arrived to verify that everything was on track. He was stunned by what he saw. By then, most of the inmates at the guest house were inebriated and the contours that separated staff from probationers became increasingly blurred. Before he could recover from the shock, a few of the drunk 'rowdies' dragged him to the dance floor. Futile attempts were made to make him drink the country liquor. This was the straw that broke the camel's back. A die-hard teetotaller and vegetarian, the staff representative, who hailed from the state of Tamil Nadu, screamed, 'Aiyyo, aiyyo' and fled to the nearest bathroom. Endless persuasion by an already harassed group leader to convince Muthusamy to unlock the door bore no results.

The group leader suddenly yelled, 'It's time to eat,' in a somewhat authoritative tone. So those of us who were still in our senses, along with those who had pretty much lost theirs, staggered out with great anticipation to have some delicious mutton curry cooked by the self-proclaimed gourmet chefs. But the sight we encountered left us shell-shocked. There were three of our colleagues, high on liquor, surrounded by half a dozen dogs who were being fed all the mutton, with a great amount of care, love and affection! Here, I naively thought the mutton was meant for us. The group leader and I decided that discretion is the better part of valour and quickly retreated into the guest house, rescued Muthusamy and quietly slept on an empty stomach, happy for the canines who enjoyed a royal feast on New Year's Eve of 1981.

The next morning, 1 January 1982, the group leader was summoned by the district collector. I decided to accompany him. Clearly, bad news travels fast. We realised this upon arriving at the spacious office of the collector, Wilfred Lakra, who admonished us for the unruly behaviour of some of our colleagues the previous night. We received an earful about the sensitivities of working in a district which was dominated by tribals. After a short yet severe lecture on etiquette and ethical behaviour, we were asked to split into groups of four and go deep into the forests of Mandla.

These were thick sal forests, with lots of wild animals. We were housed in thatched huts, fenced on four sides. We had the privilege of an armed forest guard to protect us. On the very first night of our stay, we heard bells and people singing on a hill located close to where we were staying. Naturally, our curiosity got the better of us and, despite being warned by the forest guard that it was unwise to go out at night as some wild animals may be on the prowl, we decided to go ahead and see what was happening. We set off, duly escorted by the guard, into the forest. Fortunately, it was a full-moon night and as we moved closer to the hill, the sounds became louder and more coherent.

Before us was an amazing sight, so much so that our hearts skipped a beat. We saw several young men and women, dressed in all the finery of traditional tribal wear and fresh flowers, dancing in pairs and changing partners at fairly regular intervals. We could not decipher what was going on until our guard told us that this was an annual event where young men and women would step out on a full-moon night, dance through the night, change partners, and by the time the sun began to rise, they would find their life partners and leave. It was simple, yet so modern. Witnessing such an event was indeed a unique experience. However, there was no way of confirming the authenticity of this practice.

On the next lap of our Bharat Darshan, we visited some

cities in the state of Goa, as well as Jaipur, Jodhpur and Mount Abu in Rajasthan. In Goa, there was some confusion regarding our accommodation and we ended up having two choices: abandoned and mosquito-ridden coaches in a train or open parks. Not exactly the lap of luxury, but we opted for the latter. Later, in Delhi, we also called on Prime Minister Indira Gandhi during our parliamentary attachment.

Our cooperative federation attachment was at the Anand Cooperative Dairy Federation, a world-famous example of successful cooperative efforts, pioneered by Professor Verghese Kurien. My mind, however, was on something else. I was more interested in visiting RSC in Baroda, located close to Anand.

I took a day off and went to Baroda with my friend, roommate and the current group leader, to meet Anjali who was training at the RSC. I was hesitant to leap into a proposal as no man wants to hear the dreaded 'no'. After a fair amount of cajoling from my friend, I finally proposed. I did not get an immediate response. What could it be? My mind ran in different directions. I became paranoid. Could the roadblock be 'Loo' who happened to be Anjali's roommate at RSC. Was my karma catching up with me!

I came back to Anand crestfallen. And there was more disappointing news to follow. Our state allocations had been finalised and I was to move to Tamil Nadu. I wasn't excited about being shifted to the southern state, but what I didn't know then was that the two-year stint would be an enriching and fascinating experience. Many of the fundamentals that I learnt about administration, management and leadership were inculcated in those two years. And here was one of many life lessons that I learnt: one should never be impatient and jump to conclusions based on preconceived notions. As Leo Tolstoy famously said, 'The two most powerful warriors are patience and time.'

CHAPTER FIVE

TAMIL NADU

I returned to the academy in Mussoorie after the Bharat Darshan. And after four months, I was now getting ready to leave for my district training at Tanjore (now Thanjavur) in Tamil Nadu. We were offered classes in the Tamil language as all official work there was conducted in the local language. It was a real shame that I invested more effort in the fun and frolic of academy life rather than in Tamil lessons. This would come back to haunt me.

Instead of pursuing our intellectual curiosity, my group became seriously devoted to playing 'teen patti'. This is a popular Indian card game normally played in a group of three to six persons, just like poker. Teen patti is a national pastime in India during the festival of lights, Diwali. But for this group, the occasion hardly mattered. Teen patti was an obsession for us, with most night sittings ending in the wee hours of the morning.

Leaving the academy and my friends after four months, I felt, oddly enough, neither emotional nor sad. I would miss the teen patti sessions but certainly not the academy food, which had gone from bad to worse. I boarded the night bus from Dehradun to Delhi en route to Thanjavur via Madras (now Chennai).

During my short stay in Delhi, I met Anjali. Our last meeting had left me half-paranoid, half-confused but 100 per cent hopeful (remember, I'm the 'glass is half full' kind of person). There were some indications of a positive response but nothing set in stone, so I decided to take the bull by the horns (quite literally in a sense—Anjali is a Taurean, for those inclined to put some faith in astrology), and asked her to meet my mother.

My mother was an angel. I don't say that because she is my mother. But this wonderful, kind-hearted woman would never see fault in anyone and I knew that all too well. Expectedly, that meeting went well. But *the* 'encounter' was yet to take place. I still had to contend with my father who was a strict disciplinarian. The use of the word 'strict' preceding 'disciplinarian' is quite deliberate to give you a sense of how strictly disciplinarian my father was. And when it came to marriage, discipline for my father meant love was not a precondition. Love could come later. The same evening, I asked Anjali to request her father to meet mine. The meeting was classic. My mother colluded with me and did not utter a word about her having met Anjali earlier.

My parents were staying with my brother, Rajesh, in the

Ministry of External Affairs hostel on Kasturba Gandhi Marg in Delhi, while I always stayed with my sister, Jayashree. Rajesh and I decided to stay put in the lobby while the two men met. My mother put on a blank expression and the inevitable happened. The proposal was made.

My father took it as one of the several he had received. Speaking on my behalf and with a degree of authority that was characteristically his, my father said that I did not wish to get married until my training was over. That is the line I had given him when he had asked me a few months ago as to how he should respond to the numerous marriage proposals that he had been receiving for me. Little did he realise that this one was different.

The already tense meeting took an unexpected turn when Anjali's father said, 'Look, this is not for you or me to negotiate. We only need to bless this marriage as the children have already decided.' My father, in his inimitable style, responded, 'Then why are we negotiating?' To which Anjali's father, a seasoned civil servant said, 'I was only trying to arrive at a consensus!' He left, and my brother and I went back to the apartment.

The atmosphere was explosive. My mother was being blamed for hiding and conniving with 'her' children and, needless to say, we got piercing looks. It took quite a few glasses of premium Scotch and some mouth-watering kebabs to ease the situation. I thought I had sealed the deal but did not realise that there were more hurdles to cross.

With this major issue settled, in really high spirits, I boarded the Grand Trunk Express from Delhi to Madras. This was an exhausting thirty-six-hour journey. I was so excited about how events had unfolded in Delhi that I hardly ate or slept on the train. The next evening, just a couple of hours before the train was to pull into Madras station, panic gripped me. I had been told that most people in Tamil Nadu spoke only Tamil. Having ignored my language classes at the academy, I obviously did not know a word of Tamil beyond the absolute basics, such as *Vanakkam*, *ille* and *ama*.

I had also been warned by my colleagues from Tamil Nadu that any ignorance of the local language could land me into serious trouble. My mind began racing with concern. What do I do? How do I deal with the porters at the station, the cab driver who needed to take me to the MLA hostel which was three kilometres from Madras Central Station? I was told that I would be fleeced and all I had with me were a couple of hundred rupees.

I had an idea. It was time to become acquainted with the Tamil textbooks that I had done so well to ignore at the academy. The train was hurtling towards Madras. I picked up two sentences. '*Iniki malai peyuma peyaada?*' ('Will it rain today or not?') was one. How could the cab driver not be impressed with those language skills? But surely that would not suffice. So, I looked for a second sentence. Got it, I said to myself; '*Ind nai kadikuma kadikada?*' ('Will this dog bite or not?') That is even more impressive, I thought. I recited these two sentences a dozen times as the train roared into the station.

As the train stopped, dozens of porters jumped in and started grabbing the luggage of passengers. I pointed towards my iron box and meekly followed the porter as he darted out of the train on to the platform. In seconds, we were at the imposing portico of Madras Central Station. Very quickly a cab appeared, the porter dumped my box in the boot of a rather rickety-looking cab, the old Ambassador model. I gave the porter ten rupees and we were off. So far, so good. I had managed on sign language with no reliance on Tamil at all. The driver asked me '*Enge,* Sir' or 'Where do we go?' Ah! I knew the answer to that question and I confidently said, 'MLA hostel,' a residence meant for the Members of the Legislative Assembly of Tamil Nadu. He nodded. All was on track. But then I sensed something was amiss.

I had been told that the journey to the MLA hostel from Madras Central Station was barely ten minutes. We had already been driving around for twenty minutes and there was no sign of my destination. I had to let the driver believe that I was no stranger to the area, so I put my head out of the window and looked out, on what was a day with clear blue skies, and, in a very authoritative tone, said, '*Iniki malai peyuma peyaada*?' He looked puzzled. '*Ille,* Sir, *ille,*' he responded. No, sir, no. The ride continued and I was a step closer to convincing him that I was fully literate in Tamil. But it seemed he needed more evidence. So I raised my voice as I saw a stray dog cross the road and said, '*Ind nai kadikuma kadikada*?' This had the desired effect. The cab driver thought I was stark raving mad and took me straight to my destination. Imagine sitting in a cab and worrying about a stray dog crossing the street. He put the cab into full gear, drove into the MLA hostel, threw my box on the ground and, without even taking the fare, dashed off the premises, thanking his stars that he was rid of a lunatic.

Thanjavur

The next morning, I boarded the Cholan Express from Madras to Thanjavur, my destination for district training. It involved a six-hour journey, most of which I devoted to my newfound interest in learning Tamil, a rich language, perhaps one of the oldest in India. The other highlight of the journey was a lunch served in true South Indian style.

As the clock struck noon, plantain leaves were put out on each berth and before I could understand what was happening, several servers descended on me and put out some steaming white rice, *sambhar*, some vegetables and poppadom on it. While the food looked really appetising, I lacked the art of eating with my hands. To my embarrassment, I found the *sambhar* dripping off the plantain leaf, on to the berth and then the floor of the train.

My co-passengers gave me some curious looks. They thought I had some kind of disability affecting my motor functions. One even volunteered to help me eat. Awkward moment! It was then that I understood that there is a certain technique to eating food off a plantain leaf. I also realised how culturally different we were across states and regions. I began to appreciate the real ethos and strength of India—one country, one geographical entity, a myriad of cultures, languages, customs and practices. Yet, there was the magic of unity in diversity. I truly began to appreciate what a great country I belonged to and felt very proud. This was the real India—from north to south, east to west, all woven into one great nation.

I disembarked the train and was received by a friend of one of my batchmates and taken to the Thanjavur circuit house in a rickshaw. After a quick wash, I was hosted to a 'tiffin' dinner at a nearby outlet and it is on this occasion that I was given my first lessons on how to eat and appreciate the local cuisine. I have been a fan ever since.

The next morning, I reported to the district collector, Maikandadevan, an officer from the state Civil Service promoted to the IAS. The first meeting was cold. I had the distinct feeling that I would carry the sense of being an intruder from outer space for the next nine months in Thanjavur.

Accommodation was far from five-star. I was put up in a 10x15-foot room, which had one bed, a small study table, and an attached bathroom with a toilet and a shower. A very benign, middle-aged man, Ganapathi, was assigned to be my man Friday. I was entirely dependent on *sappad* or food from the outside. Five days a week, a Tamil teacher would tutor me. Having learnt my lesson on the very first day of my arrival, I now took the language classes very seriously. This held me in good stead as I managed to clear my Tamil language examinations in one shot.

I was handed over by the collector to one of his deputies, Thangavelu, who was a considerate person and put me through the rigours of training in a thorough and meticulous manner. I was even assigned some court work and would pass judgments on some petty crime cases such as stealing of coconuts or bicycles. I felt mighty pleased pronouncing judgments and determining the quantum of punishment, which would be a paltry 200 to 300 rupees. I did get carried away on one occasion and threatened the offender with a two-month jail sentence until I was politely told by my support staff that this was clearly beyond my remit. My staff in Tamil Nadu was extremely well-mannered and soft-spoken—like all the people in this part of the country. This is not something I would say for the region I belonged to and where I would eventually land up to work. There is a huge respect for hierarchy and the line of command in Tamil Nadu.

The President of India, Giani Zail Singh, was to visit the coastal town of Nagapattinam and I found that I had not been given a specific role. I decided to assert myself and reached the collector's residence when he was about to leave for the venue, which was a two-hour drive from the district headquarters. Reluctantly, he let me sit with him and I felt absolutely thrilled—not so much at the prospect of meeting the President of India but at being driven in the collector's car. The visit of the President was relatively uneventful except that I was introduced to him and shook his hands. My list of celebrity sightings was growing.

The rest of the district training exposed me to a well-organised administrative structure in Tamil Nadu. As part of the district training, we were expected to write a 'Village Report'. It gave me an insight into the level of development which was truly remarkable with respect to safe drinking water and roads. The mid-day meal scheme for schoolchildren was meticulously supervised. Land records were maintained in an orderly manner. The presence of the administration in terms of visits to old-age homes, jails and shelters for destitute women was impressive. Reports were made to the state government on a monthly basis and officers spent three to four days a month touring the district, all signs of a well-oiled administrative machinery. This was something I failed to see in later years when I worked in the states of Uttar Pradesh and Uttarakhand. Tamil Nadu was indeed a great learning experience for me and I cherish the time spent there to this day.

Dindigul

After Phase II at the academy, which was largely devoted to sharing experiences from the district training, I was posted as sub-collector at Dindigul, a sub-division of Madurai district. Generally, sub-collector is the first posting as an IAS officer after the completion of training. Dindigul was an important sub-division and a geographically large one. Later, it was upgraded to a district headed by a collector.

I reached Dindigul, via Madurai, in the summer of 1983. Unlike my previous accommodation, I now had the privilege of living in a beautiful, hundred-year-old stone house with a tiled roof, surrounded by lots of greenery and a tennis court. The recreation room was equipped with a table tennis table, a small library, a courtroom and my camp office. In short, the setting was regal. The luxury was capped with my own jeep and driver, and a domestic help to ensure my life was well organised. In spite of this rosy picture, I had two prickly situations to manage: one personal, the other official.

On the personal side, two of my aunts had passed away in September 1982 and in March 1983. In our family, the loss of a close relative meant that we had to respect a one-year mourning period during which time no celebrations, including weddings, could take place. When my elder aunt suddenly passed away, my father told me that my wedding would need to be postponed beyond September 1983. I agreed. Tradition was important to my family, especially to my father.

Bearing this in mind, my wedding was fixed for 24 October 1983. But tragically, I lost another aunt in March 1983. So, should the wedding now be postponed beyond March 1984? I decided to draw the line and broached my father. He hinted about a further postponement but this time I told him that in a large family such as ours this could continue to happen. I wasn't being pessimistic. It was a mere statement of fact. It was also unfair to Anjali and her family. He understood and we agreed to have a very simple wedding—minus the frills—on the scheduled date.

On the work front, I was dealing with a boss known to be a firebrand and a very strict taskmaster, bordering on authoritarian. Not all collectors were as strict with their staff. But unfortunately for me, this was the reputation of 'Amma'. My boss was famous for her weekly meetings with the sub-collectors and block development officers in her charge. These were Monday meetings scheduled at her residence at 9 a.m. but invariably they began three hours late. We would sit there like lambs awaiting slaughter. What made it worse was the presence of a large blackboard with dusters and plenty of chalk ready for Amma to take us to task, and quite literally so. Fear and trepidation would grip us as the clock neared noon but no one would say a word. Suddenly, there would be sounds of people running frenetically: Amma was on her way. The paths were cleared and then the 'shush' of the curtain which separated us from Amma's residence would be pulled aside. Amma was here! Forty-odd people would jump to their feet and wish her as children wish their teachers, in total unison and heads lowered as an act of subservience. Amma would barely acknowledge these overtures. With a wave of her hand, we would be signalled to sit down and the 'class' would then begin.

You would think that having spent some years as a student of St. Columba's School in New Delhi, traumatised at times by the overtly strict disciplinary approach of the Irish brothers, I would have been prepared for the worst. But this class took the cake. In a few seconds, Amma would assume the role of a teacher, stand in front of the blackboard and start asking questions in a random manner. God help those who could not answer questions pertaining to the norms applicable for programmes implemented under the aegis of the District Rural Development Agency, or some basic data about the district. They were met with a duster flying in their direction, which they had the choice to either catch or deftly deflect.

This kind of rigorous interrogation would go on for three to four hours. Luckily, I was spared the duster. In fact, towards the close of my tenure, Amma even rewarded me with a leather briefcase and 10 grams of gold which Anjali quickly converted into a band.

Throughout my career, I have observed different styles of administration. Amma's was that of a strong administrator with an eye for detail; today's style of administration is largely flippant and superficial. Amma had the time and energy to devote to key developmental issues. Today's administrators are too caught up in managing local politicians, law-and-order situations and, of course, dodging social media bullets.

Amma was also famous for surprise visits to sub-divisions. She would announce her destination only after the car was in motion. On one such occasion, she got into the car, after dinner, and did not announce where she wanted to go. No one dared to ask. So, her driver took the road to Dindigul. He looked back once in a while but Amma was fast asleep. It was at that time that he panicked and asked the *dafedar* (peon/orderly) to message me on the walkie-talkie, there being no mobile phones, that Amma was arriving. I used to work until late but this was quite an unnerving message to receive close to midnight.

The tahsildar, or the revenue officer, was woken out of his slumber and asked to get Amma's room ready in the government guest house. I took my jeep and rushed to the guest house as well but there was no sign of her for the next hour or so. We started to get worried. Then a low voice reported on the walkie-talkie that though they had reached Dindigul they were not entering the guest house as Amma was still fast asleep. Finally, she arrived, barely looked at the tahsildar and me, and headed for her room. The door was slammed. We were on our customary ten-minute wait until things settled down. But then we heard the banging of a door and loud screams from Amma.

Amma was locked in the bathroom as the precariously held handle fell when she closed the door. The search began for a carpenter. It was well past midnight by now. Amma's shouting and screaming got more and more shrill. There was pandemonium. The guest house in charge and the civil engineer both rushed to the scene and finally the door of the bathroom opened. Amma looked exhausted. A couple of suspension orders were dictated and we left. Imagine this style of functioning today. Amma would probably be hauled up before a human rights body or accused of indulging in unethical behaviour. The pros and cons of her approach can be debated but Amma ran the district with an iron fist and Madurai was a standout in terms of performance. There was a lot to learn from Amma, and I have no hesitation in saying that I adopted several facets of her administrative style. It is for my juniors to pronounce judgement on whether I imbibed her impetuous and at times maverick style as well.

My stint in Dindigul was an extremely enjoyable and fulfilling one. I learnt the ropes of administration and became quite fluent in Tamil. Three months into the job, I got married in a simple yet elegant wedding ceremony in Delhi. In June

1983, Anjali had qualified for the IAS and had managed to get just four days off to get married. Given the short time at our disposal, we decided to forego our honeymoon and instead spend time with my parents. It remains a lifelong regret, as Anjali's father had booked us at the Lake Palace Hotel in Udaipur. These moments do not come back but one should never live with regrets.

I accompanied Anjali to Mussoorie, where we stayed in her ancestral home, Savitri Villa. She would leave for the academy each morning at 7 a.m. and I would catch up with her later in the day. Starting from day one, we learnt how to respect each other's professional lives, make the necessary adjustments and yet remain totally bonded. It has been difficult and challenging at times, but after thirty-seven years I can say that we have succeeded, with Anjali doing the heavy lifting most of the time. Managing a profession, a family, a house and a rather demanding husband has been no easy task for Anjali, but she has more than lived up to the challenge.

Between November 1983 and May 1984, Anjali made several trips to Chennai/Dindigul. The Mussoorie–Dehradun–Delhi–Chennai/Dindigul trips, to and fro in two to three days, were tough to say the least. In December 1983, Anjali was allotted the Uttar Pradesh cadre. We had a choice; as per the rules we could be allocated the same cadre so she could come to Tamil Nadu or I could go to Uttar Pradesh. By then I was very well settled in Tamil Nadu and was not inclined to leave. Anjali was supportive of this. But one episode kept coming back to my mind—my meeting with the chief revenue administrator of Tamil Nadu, who is ranked next to the chief secretary.

My whole batch had called on him. We were a large batch of ten. Five of us were not from Tamil Nadu. As soon as we settled down for our meeting, he said, 'Now tell me who are the foreigners?' We all looked shell-shocked. Who was he referring to as 'foreigners'? Seeing our nonplussed expression, he went on to explain: 'I mean the ones who do not belong to Tamil Nadu.' Meekly, five of us raised our hands. I asked myself how I was going to work for the next thirty-six years in a state that would treat me as a foreigner. I opted for Uttar Pradesh. Just to clarify, my colleagues who continued in Tamil Nadu have never felt that way but the incident with the chief revenue administrator did leave an indelible mark on my psyche. I found myself on the train from Chennai to Delhi en route to Moradabad district, where I was posted as subdivisional magistrate and where Anjali would do her district training.

CHAPTER SIX

UTTAR PRADESH

Moradabad

On 4 June 1984, Anjali and I boarded the Delhi to Benares (now Varanasi) Ganga Yamuna Express to our new assignment in Moradabad. With its four million inhabitants, the city is famous for its huge export of brass handicrafts to the rest of the world, earning the nickname 'Brass City', Peetal Nagri in the local language.

Sadly for us, there was no one to receive us in spite of several messages that had been sent to the district magistrate's (DM) office transmitting the details of our arrival. So, there we were, two young officers arriving for our first posting in the coveted state of Uttar Pradesh, yet clueless about our next move. Uttar Pradesh was the dream first posting, a state comprising 120 million people, which had given birth to all but one prime minister of India until then. Officers who were lucky enough to have worked in that state held a great amount of authority in the corridors of power in Delhi.

Starry-eyed, we arrived to be confronted with the brute reality of the state, its politicians and its bureaucracy—not to mention the complex mix of social and economic issues. Little did I realise, coming from Tamil Nadu, with its very well-organised, sedate and peaceful style of administration, that I would be confronted with the polar opposite of my previous posting.

We loaded our joint belongings—now two iron boxes—onto a hand-driven rickshaw. There was one immediate problem though: we had no idea where to go. It was getting dark and western Uttar Pradesh was not reputed to be the safest place in India. We asked the rickshaw puller to take us to the nearest government guest house. He took us to an abandoned Awas Vikas or Housing Board guest house on the main G.T. Road, located on the outskirts of Moradabad. The rickshaw puller left and we saw no signs of life.

It was pitch-dark now. I mustered the courage to go to the backyard and found a candle burning in a small room. I looked in and saw a dishevelled man cooking his dinner on firewood. Confession time: I was stressed. Had I been alone, roughing it for a night would have been fine, but Anjali was with me.

My voice breaking, I asked the man whether we could spend the night in the guest house. He sent a confused look my way, pointing out that the guest house had not been in use for several years. Unfortunately, we didn't have much choice as the only other option was to spend the night outdoors.

Reluctantly, he opened a door of the guest house and dumped our luggage in the first room. He lit a candle and gave it to us and warned us to close the door as this area was unsafe. We quickly slammed the old, rickety and creaking door.

The bad dream soon turned into a nightmare. Huge rats, the size of mini porcupines, and lizards that looked like monsters were running helter-skelter in the room. They sensed intruders in their otherwise peaceful existence. Petrified, we decided to sit on our boxes and spend the night making sure the rats did not crawl over us. So, our first night in the most powerful state of India was not picture-prefect: no food, no water, no sleep. Welcome to the IAS ...

The next morning, totally drained of energy, we set off for the DM's office where we were expected to report for duty. As we arrived at the gate of the collector's residence, where his camp office was located, a reluctant guard at the gate needed to be persuaded to let us in. In Uttar Pradesh there is a tradition of DMs having a fully functional office in their residence; a 'working from home' concept which would be deployed across the world thirty-five years later during the COVID-19 pandemic.

We entered the premises of the DM's residence which had an impressive half-a-kilometre driveway, with manicured gardens that led to a majestic-looking house. The trauma of the night before began to fade as we went into a dream world of what could possibly be our existence a few years down the road. But that was going to be a long and difficult journey to traverse.

We were met by the private secretary to the collector, the 'steno babu' who behaved and posed as the next most important person after the DM. We were seated on a bench and asked to wait for a call from the DM. After a two-hour wait—still with no sleep, food or water—we finally got our audience with the man. Our first impression of the DM, Vijai Sharma, whom we later called 'Jackson', was that he was a stern-looking, matter-of-fact person who was all about business. He gave us a piercing look and probably thought 'two more to deal with'.

The DM looked totally unimpressed with my background of having worked in Tamil Nadu. There was a world of difference between the two states. As different as night and day in terms of the priorities and challenges an administrator would encounter. Jackson made no bones about conveying this to me.

A very trite conversation followed our introduction to a swashbuckling, strapping young man, donning a pair of sunglasses and a revolver in his hip pocket, with a well-manicured beard to complete the look. Anjali and I were to later nickname him as 'Alfa'. Alfa seemed to be the next in command. He was the city magistrate and belonged to the Provincial Civil Service. He was told to lodge us somewhere and basically supervise our settling-down formalities. Alfa appeared to be an arrogant and abrasive person. Little did he realise that he would meet me in another capacity a few years later. It is always wise to remember that very often you meet the same people going down the ladder as you meet when going up.

Our next port of call was the divisional commissioner, who oversaw the work of four to five districts but is usually a figurehead with the real authority vested in the office of the DM. The divisional commissioner, Mohinder Singh, a Sikh gentleman, was a benign and fatherly figure. One look at us and he realised that all was not well. He inquired about how we had fared so far and was absolutely livid to hear about our plight. He promptly picked up the phone and gave an earful to the DM, saying, 'We simply cannot treat our young officers like this.'

Thereafter, things began to move. We were allotted a one-room accommodation in the transit officers' quarters. It was unfurnished. Anjali and I had ten thousand rupees—gifts received at our wedding reception. We quickly depleted our earnings, buying a small Kelvinator fridge, one bed and a few utensils. That night we slept on a bed and in the comfort of a ceiling fan. It felt like a five-star treat to us after the traumatic experience merely twenty-four hours ago.

'Welcome to Uttar Pradesh' resounded in our ears as we embarked on one of our most testing, trying yet rich and varied experiences in India's Hindi heartland. Work began in earnest from the next day. My year-long stint in Moradabad can be broken up into three distinct parts: the communal situation, Indira Gandhi's assassination and its aftermath, and the style and nature of the administrative machinery in its day-to-day functioning.

The 1980s in India were marked by unfortunate and often violent communal clashes, generally between Hindus and Muslims. Perhaps the most serious and noteworthy was the incident that took place in Moradabad on 13 August 1980, when the police opened fire on a crowd of nearly 80,000 that had gathered at the Eidgah (an open space near a mosque where Muslims offer prayers) on the occasion of Eid-ul-Fitr. This incident, which resulted in the death of 300 persons on the spot, is the subject of much conjecture. One version is that this was not a communal incident but a case of police brutality on an unarmed and hapless congregation. Another, more acceptable, theory is that a pig, which was later to be called 'item' by the DM, suddenly emerged at the Eidgah, considered as sacrilege by the Muslim community, leading to an uproar and subsequent stampede. The congregation responded with stone-throwing and arson. The police fired indiscriminately. Moradabad burned.

Clearly, Moradabad was still sitting on a tinderbox with palpable tension between Hindus and Muslims when I arrived to serve in the district in 1984. It is important to understand that Moradabad had a population of close to half a million, with the two communities having equal share. This is well above the national average of the Muslim population of 15 per cent.

While the artisans of Moradabad's world-renowned brassware industry are mainly Muslims, the financiers, traders and exporters are generally Hindus, leading some to say that '*Mussalman kamata hai; Hindu khata hai*' (the Muslims work and the Hindus enjoy the fruits of their labour). I was slowly understanding why the DM looked so tense and so committed to details besides referring to the 'pig' as 'item'. Even the use of the word 'pig' was considered sacrilege.

Initially, I was posted at an outlying sub-division, Thakurdwara, approximately fifty kilometres from the district headquarters, located in the Terai region of India, just twelve kilometres from the industrial town of Kashipur, now part of the state of Uttarakhand. Anjali was stationed at Moradabad and I would commute on a daily basis. The DM tasked me to find a solution to a problem which had existed for the last forty years. This related to settling a route for the Tazia procession which the Muslims, generally Shias, take on the occasion of Moharram, a set of commemoration rituals observed in the first month of the Islamic calendar. It was a vexed problem as the Hindu community had opposed the traditional route set for the procession.

I persevered with both communities for days. It was my first brush with negotiations, a challenging task fraught with the danger of upsetting the status quo that had existed for forty years. But I had to succeed. It was my first test. My perseverance paid off. Both communities agreed but, in such situations, nothing can be taken as a done deal unless it actually materialises—seeing is believing. I waited for D-day with bated breath.

The procession came down the traditional route and there was no opposition from the Hindus. Everything passed peacefully. My first success in the state of Uttar Pradesh but that was not enough to impress my boss. He waited for another occasion to test me and it came in the form of flash floods in Thakurdwara.

I was woken up at 2 a.m. by the DM and ordered to leave for Thakurdwara immediately. I left in an open jeep, under pouring rain, with a driver, Thapa, at the wheels. Sadly, Thapa was drunk. Midway to Thakurdwara, my jeep almost got swept off by a swollen Ramganga River—another near-death experience. We reached Thakurdwara drenched but miraculously intact. With a population of around 40,000 people, my task was cut out. Rescue, relief and rehabilitation were the priorities. Most of the population had abandoned their homes and taken shelter at higher levels. They needed food and water while they waited to be rescued.

Assisted by a small number of officials, I set off on a boat, laden with food, clean drinking water, candles and matchsticks, and some cash to hand over to stranded persons. The DM arrived at 8 a.m., briefly assessed the situation, gave some instructions and left. Apparently, he was satisfied with the rescue and relief works. It gave me a sense of contentment. I had the trust of the DM. There was no attempt to micromanage and it was a perfect case of delegation. The flood waters subsided in a couple of days and I returned to the headquarters to find a one-line transfer order on my table. I had been moved to Moradabad as the subdivisional magistrate (SDM). I was comforted by the thought that I had won the confidence of the DM. The transfer was a subtle way of conveying his appreciation.

Soon after I assumed charge as SDM, Moradabad, preparations were underway to celebrate the festival of Eid-ul-Fitr. This was always a grim reminder of the events of 1980. The administration was gripped with a sense of paranoia. It was at this time that the DM first introduced the concept of 'item'. He asked us to conduct a survey of all the 'items' in the district. This was no mean task considering there were countless of them. He wanted each one of them rounded up and kept in 'custody' until Eid-ul-Fitr was over. Indeed, a mammoth task but we got down to doing the impossible.

We gave an all-clear report to the DM on the evening before Eid-ul-Fitr. The instructions were crystal clear. Not a single 'item' should surface near the Eidgah, preferably even Moradabad town. All set, Anjali and I reported for duty at the Eidgah at 4 a.m. So did Alfa and the superintendent of police (SP), Moradabad city—all the troops at our disposal. All drains (where the 'items' love to live) close to the Eidgah had been covered with asbestos sheets and the length and breadth of the Eidgah was being patrolled. The clock chimed 6 a.m. and not an 'item' in sight. The Eid-ul-Fitr prayers were scheduled to start at 9 a.m. and the crowds would start pouring in soon after 8 a.m. We still had two hours. So, we decided to have a cup of tea and some biscuits in a nearby dhaba. But the peace of the morning and our tea break was broken by a huge commotion.

An 'item' had been spotted and we could see a whole posse of policemen, led by SP Ranjan Dwivedi and the city magistrate, chasing the 'item', which turned out to be a rather strenuous exercise with this very agile and slippery animal. Finally, after a half-kilometre chase, one of the policemen just took the plunge and with a hop, skip and jump worthy of the Olympics, flung himself on to the 'item'. The 'item' went ballistic but the policeman would not give up. Others joined him and took control of the situation. The 'item' was bundled into a closed vehicle and driven off in style to some unknown destination several kilometres away from the Eidgah. The DM and the senior SP arrived. No one dared to tell them what had just transpired. The Eid-ul-Fitr celebrations went off peacefully. One more feather in the DM's cap.

Soon, I understood that the communal situation in Moradabad was fragile. In a country that prided itself on being secular, why was this the case? Something to ponder. In retrospect, I think it was the consistent policy of the political parties to treat the minorities, in particular the Muslims, as a vote bank. A deliberate policy of appeasement was followed.

The administration would receive direct messages from the prime minister's office regarding arrangements for Muslim festivals but not for Hindu festivals. This was not equality, it was appeasement. Several years of unabashedly following this policy gave birth to resentment and anger amongst the majority Hindu community. This anger would find a political voice in the coming years. The contrarian view is that the minority community in India remains socially and economically backward and deserves special attention. Food for thought for historians in the years to come. I humbly offer it as a point of view from a young administrator's brush with 'secular' India.

The 31st of October 1984 seemed like any ordinary day. I was attending a meeting convened by the divisional commissioner at 10 a.m. to discuss the organisation of a major sports event he was planning and for which I had been identified as the focal point. Fully armed with all the facts and details, I arrived at the commissioner's office at 9.50 a.m. The meeting started at 10 a.m. sharp and we got into the logistics of organising an inter-district event which would span three days. An hour or so into the meeting, a messenger came into the room and passed a slip of paper to the commissioner. Little did I realise at that moment that India's history had changed.

The commissioner read the piece of paper but looked remarkably unruffled on the surface so as not to create panic. The meeting was concluded rather hastily. He told us to go straight to the DM's office. I jumped into my jeep and drove to his camp office. An unusual number of vehicles were parked in the compound. Something was amiss, but I had no clue of the gravity of the news I was about to receive.

The DM was already conducting a meeting and the atmosphere was very tense and serious. I was still not aware of the subject matter until, with a very grave expression on his face, the DM said, 'Prime Minister Indira Gandhi has been assassinated.' We were stunned. The details began to pour in. At 9.20 a.m., Mrs Gandhi was shot thirty-three times by her two Sikh bodyguards at her official residence as she stepped out to meet people gathered for the daily *darshan*. She was rushed to the All India Institute of Medical Sciences. In spite of the doctors doing their best to save her, Mrs Gandhi was declared dead at 10.50 a.m. All India Radio announced the news at 11 a.m., identifying her assassins. The country went into a tizzy.

What was the background to Mrs Gandhi's assassination? It was an already troubled decade in terms of communal violence. In addition to this, the early part of the 1980s saw the violent Sikh separatist Khalistan movement which sought independence from India. The separatists were led by Jarnail Singh Bhindranwale and were holed up in perhaps the most sacred of Sikh shrines in India, the Golden Temple in Amritsar, Punjab. The prime minister ordered Operation Bluestar, which involved a military operation to flush out the terrorists from the Golden Temple. Carried out between 1 and 8 June 1984, it resulted in the death of Bhindranwale and several of his compatriots and freed the temple from militants. But this act of military intrusion in the holy precincts of the Golden Temple did not go down well with the Sikh community. For them it was a brutal attack on their religion. Several protests, some of a violent nature, were felt in most parts of northern India. Anjali and I had arrived in Moradabad in the midst of this crisis. However, the situation was contained. Four months later, Mrs Gandhi was assassinated in an act of vengeance by her own Sikh bodyguards.

What followed Mrs Gandhi's assassination will always remain a blot on India's history. The whole of north India, with its epicentre in Delhi, was rocked by anti-Sikh riots. Uttar Pradesh along with Punjab, Haryana, Madhya Pradesh and Bihar were the hardest hit. The next four days saw the targeted and brutal killing of Sikhs, a community known for its loyalty, valour and commitment to the national cause, that too in the capital city of the country, for absolutely no fault of theirs. Some refer to these senseless acts as the 'Sikh genocide'. Whatever terminology we may like to use, we need to hang our heads in shame and forever seek forgiveness from this gallant and brave community that has continued to remain an integral part of India, contributing to its diversity and unity.

In Moradabad, the situation was extremely tense. Most cities and towns of Uttar Pradesh were under curfew. The administration worked day and night to maintain peace, and under the very able leadership of the DM we managed to do so. I began to understand from my boss that the devil is in the detail, and meticulous planning is a must to achieve success, particularly in dealing with such complex situations. I learnt the art—and science—of maintaining a checklist, which I do until this day. Never count on your memory, I say to myself and my staff as I prepare a fresh checklist every morning.

Rajiv Gandhi, Mrs Gandhi's elder son, was sworn in as prime minister the same night. National elections were held soon after and in the sympathy wave generated over the assassination, the Indian National Congress won a thumping 404 of the 514 seats for which elections were held. The Bharatiya Janata Party (BJP) won only two seats. Astonishing how the political landscape could change so dramatically in under three decades. A sure indication of the very healthy and thriving democracy that is India.

In our own small world of Moradabad, elections for the Parliament were followed by elections to the state Legislative Assembly. I was the returning officer for the Moradabad seat. The election assumed a communal nature as the Muslim League candidate lost to a relatively unknown Congress candidate by a wafer-thin margin of 600 votes. The Muslim League demanded a recount. There were no electronic voting machines and counting was done manually, one vote at a time. It used to take a couple of days to complete the counting process.

As we were expected to announce the trends after every round of counting, the tension was palpable with each round showing a neck-and-neck contest between the Muslim League and Congress candidates. As I announced the final result, the Muslim League supporters vociferously asked for a recount. As a returning officer, the decision was entirely mine. The Congress, on the other hand, wanted me to hand over the paper announcing the result. I held back and thought carefully. Given the already volatile atmosphere, a recount could lead to scrutiny or objection on every single vote cast. It could take days. Meanwhile, communal tension would rise. I had to do something which would be in perfect order according to the rules and procedure. I also needed to bear in mind the external environment.

I passed a speaking order and rejected the request for a recount. Chants of 'SDM Naresh Prasad *murdabad*' filled the air from the supporters of the Muslim League candidate. Minor scuffles began to take place between the Muslim League and Congress supporters. The situation was tense. I collected my papers, leaving the police to handle the situation, and went straight to meet the DM. He turned around and, in a matter-of-fact manner, asked me, 'But why did you not order a recount?' I was flabbergasted. No one was around when I had to make a crucial decision and now I was being questioned. I gave my reasons and left. Another lesson learnt. Always guard your flanks. Be sure of your rules and procedures as success has many friends but failure has none. The Muslim League went to the high court on the matter and involved their national leaders. I was dubbed pro-Hindu but then it all petered out and they did not pursue the matter any further.

As is evident, the life of a civil servant serving in the field in Uttar Pradesh is largely devoted to maintaining peace and tranquillity. Development quite obviously takes a backseat. This was in sharp contrast to Tamil Nadu where the focus was on development. Amma and Jackson, though very different personalities, had very similar styles of functioning; both were hardworking, diligent and devoted to their work, both believed in taking everything seriously and went into the minutest details of every issue. But their priorities differed owing to the milieu they worked in. I was indeed fortunate to have served under two such inspiring officers who have left a lasting imprint on me.

As if there wasn't enough excitement in my Moradabad

assignment, towards the end of my posting, I woke up one morning to be informed that five hardened criminals had escaped from the city jail, looted a train near the Moodha Pandey railway station and were shot dead in a scuffle with police who had arrived at the site of the crime. Under the law, deaths occurring in such circumstances require a *panchnama,* a document explaining the facts of the case in the presence of five independent witnesses. The *panchnama* has to be conducted in the presence of a magistrate. Since Moodha Pandey, which is eighteen kilometres from Moradabad and eight kilometres before Rampur, fell within my sub-division, I was hauled out of bed at 5 a.m. to reach the spot. Anjali decided to accompany me. At that moment, I did not realise that my decision would have some far-reaching consequences.

The day was breaking and a large crowd had collected by the time we reached the scene of the crime. The police officers related the whole incident to me in graphic detail. I was then made to inspect the bodies of the five men strewn close to each other but in different directions. It was a nauseating sight. Anjali followed me quietly. I got down to recording a report, largely the police version of the incident. Five meek-looking villagers put their thumb impressions on this report. This took about two excruciating hours. While trying to make sense of the report, talking to both the police and a few bystanders, I did not realise that Anjali had wandered off from the scene of the incident and been talking to a few more 'independent' witnesses. My work over, we headed back home. It was quite an ordeal—so much so that we were speechless on the drive back. In Anjali's mind, though, thoughts were brewing.

In those days, officers had to maintain a daily diary during their period of district training which would be submitted to the DM on a weekly basis before its onward transmission to the course director at the academy. Anjali submitted her diary as usual. Soon after, the DM summoned me. From the corner of my eye, I recognised Anjali's diary lying on his desk. He passed the diary to me and asked me to read the recordings of the previous week. I was puzzled.

I realised that Anjali had dubbed the entire Moodha Pandey incident as a 'fake encounter' based on her conversations with 'independent' villagers while I had been working on the report. A fake encounter has serious repercussions for the administration, in particular the policemen involved, who could be charged with murder. I returned the diary to the DM and looked at him quizzically. What did he expect me to do?

The DM asked me if I could get her to change or delete the paragraph relating to the encounter. That put me on the spot. I thought for a moment and politely declined. The reason is twofold. Firstly, Anjali and I had a mutual understanding that we would never interfere in each other's official work. Secondly, I knew first-hand Anjali's trademark capacity to call a spade a spade. I advised the DM to speak with her directly. He heeded my advice and the matter was resolved through a protracted process of discussions between the trainee and the trainer. This episode quite obviously left a lasting impression on the DM as he ended up putting a comment in Anjali's diary: 'This is the diary of Anne Frank!'

My one-year stint in Moradabad was truly a baptism by fire. A year that will forever remain etched in my memory.

Aligarh

In July 1985, I was posted as chief development officer with the rank of additional district magistrate, in charge of all development work related to rural Aligarh. I was thrilled at being promoted to the senior scale of the IAS. Anjali was posted as subdivisional magistrate, Aligarh.

The first recorded history of Aligarh goes back to the establishment of the Aligarh Fort in the sixteenth century. Today, Aligarh is a university town, notable as the seat of the Aligarh Muslim University, which was founded here as the Muhammadan Anglo-Oriental College in 1875. This was seen as a culmination of the movement led by Sir Syed Ahmed Khan to establish a modern system of education for Muslims during the later decades of the nineteenth century.

In terms of demographics, Aligarh was pretty similar to Moradabad, with Muslims constituting 45 per cent of the population. It too was a communally sensitive town which had witnessed several skirmishes and riots between Hindus and Muslims. Aligarh is famous for its lock industry and brass hardware sculpture. While the artisans were generally Muslims, the financiers and exporters were mostly Hindus, signalling interdependence and coexistence.

I had hoped that my stint in Aligarh would be solely devoted to development work but it was not to be. From time to time, I was roped into law-and-order situations. That said, my focus remained largely on rural development which I thoroughly enjoyed from day one. Aligarh was a large district and, for purposes of rural development, was administratively divided into seventeen blocks headed by block development officers. There were also elected, public representatives in each block, called *pramukhs*. The district had two elected Members of Parliament (MPs), one nominated MP, eleven Members of the Legislative Assembly (MLAs), one of whom happened to be the home minister of Uttar Pradesh. It was a district dominated by the opposition Lok Dal Party (LDP) with most of the MLAs belonging to the party, while the MPs were all from the Congress party, which was in power both at the centre and at the state level. In short, a very complex political milieu requiring very sensitive handling of all issues, in particular development.

I had a large office in the imposing Zilla Parishad building in the heart of the town. I also had a chauffeur-driven car, a retinue of staff and was allotted a nice, independent house with a garden. I actually began to feel 'senior' at the age of twenty-eight. On the very first day, I launched into a detailed briefing from my staff about the status of ongoing projects but very little was said about the financial allocations. At my insistence, I was presented with a chart of the block-wise distribution of funds. At the very first glance it appeared to be totally skewed. Nearly 50 per cent of the funds had been earmarked for the constituency of the home minister, while the rest was shared by ten other MLAs. This was clearly unacceptable. The very first official order that I passed in Aligarh district was to divide the funds allocated for the district equally among the fourteen blocks. For me, this was logical and fair but little did I realise or understand the storm I was creating for myself.

The same night I received a call from the home minister's office. I was being summoned for a 9 p.m. meeting at the minister's residence. As a probationer in the academy, I was taught that I could decline such a request as public representatives were expected to meet civil servants only in their offices or in the government guest house when meeting after office hours. But that was the theory. I was also taught to use good judgement and since it was the first such summon, I decided not to pick a fight.

I went to the minister's residence and waited a while before I got my audience. He sounded angry and upset. Word about the redistribution of funds equally to all blocks had come as a shock to him. He could not contain himself. I listened quietly and then told him in no uncertain terms that what I had done was totally fair. As is the case with most bullies, when he realised what he had said was like water off a duck's back, he decided to calm down and cajole me. I stood my ground. Finally, in exasperation he said that he would have Anjali and me transferred to two different places of posting.

With a blank expression, I drew his attention to a recent directive issued by Prime Minister Rajiv Gandhi that in order to encourage more women into the Civil Service, married couples, to the extent possible, 'shall be posted together'. Having dealt with that, I gave him the parting shot. I said, 'You can go ahead and post us out of Aligarh. If you post us to the eastern part of Uttar Pradesh, I will be closer to my parents [who were residing in Patna, the capital of the state of Bihar], in Aligarh I am close to Delhi, where all my relatives reside, and I do not mind the central part of UP either.' He looked at me, nonplussed and hapless. I went on to work in Aligarh for the next three years, well beyond my tenure of two years.

The lesson learnt was that if civil servants do not get too attached to their positions and places of posting, they can work in an upright and fearless manner. It is only when they seek favours from their political masters that they have to go down the path of subservience and even cowardice. It is my conviction that it is not right to blame politicians for the acts of omission and commission—we have only ourselves to blame. I stand by this belief until this day.

My decision to allocate funds uniformly across the district had a most unexpected consequence. In stark contrast to the fury of the powerful home minister, the other public representatives, cutting across party lines, were most appreciative of my decision. These public representatives included MPs and MLAs from the ruling Congress party, to which the minister belonged, as well as the opposition leaders—one of whom, Kalyan Singh, went on to become the chief minister of the state five years later when the BJP came to power in the state. I had learnt my first lessons in impartiality and neutrality being the basic tenets of any good administration and this would hold me in good stead throughout my career.

I immersed myself in development-related work. My days began with meeting people. Success in this job meant keeping one's ear to the ground. The numbers grew from single digits to over one hundred a day. I would pass orders, in writing, on the spot and hand over the paper to the applicant. Each order was time-bound. There was resistance from my staff as they saw the old system of establishing middlemen collapse. My logic was plain and simple. Who could be more interested in getting a job done than the applicants themselves? And the moment a deadline passed and a job was not done, the applicant would come back to me. That was the simplest and surest way to monitor the implementation of my orders. As to the endless arguments put up by my staff that such levels of transparency were not appropriate, I would tell them that what we were addressing were basic amenities such as roads, electricity and drinking water, which rural India was entitled to close to forty years after Independence. We were not talking about rocket science or state secrets such as defence and intelligence. It seemed to work as I had a most fulfilling period on this front. But someone was still agitating to get me posted out of the district.

In 1987, northern India faced a severe drought. Aligarh was badly impacted. I drew up a detailed contingency plan to deal with the situation. This plan focused on providing employment to all able-bodied persons, safe drinking water for residents, and water and fodder for cattle. We launched a massive self-employment programme through the construction of soft infrastructure such as link roads for villages and digging up of ponds. The next challenge was to ensure safe sources of water. I discovered that India Mark II pumps could be installed and operationalised in three to four days. The whole district was mapped and the pumps installed. They served two purposes:

providing safe drinking water for residents and a lifeline for cattle. All able-bodied persons were employed, received wages, food or cash in their hands and at the same time, we created necessary infrastructure. Aligarh was declared as a model district in handling the drought. The public representatives were very appreciative except one: the home minister.

The home minister was a close confidant of the chief minister of the state. He had complained bitterly about me. He wanted Anjali and me out of the district. My two-year term was coming to an end. Anjali was expected to move out on her promotion to the senior scale. The chief minister, Veer Bahadur Singh, decided to make a visit to Aligarh to gauge the situation personally. The atmosphere in the meeting hall was tense. Just that morning the newspapers had reported that Anjali had been transferred out of Aligarh. By implication, I would also move out. The home minister had a smirk on his face.

The meeting began in earnest. The chief minister undertook a very detailed review. He said that the prime minister was likely to make a surprise visit to districts close to Delhi to inspect the drought relief works. Next, the home minister took the floor and without launching a frontal attack on me said that the chief minister needed to post a capable CDO to the district as I was going to move out. He would regret that statement given what transpired over the next hour.

Public representatives, one after the other, cutting across party lines stood up and told the chief minister that I should not leave the district at this critical juncture. They also pointed out that if Anjali was transferred, quite naturally I would leave with her. The chief minister turned to the home minister and in a tone which was not exactly low or mild said, 'But you had told me that this officer is no good; you seem to have no judgement.' The home minister was speechless. Next, the chief minister asked to speak to the appointments secretary in Lucknow. The landline was in the next room. He got up in a huff and left the meeting hall, spoke to the appointments secretary and asked him to stay Anjali's transfer order. The clear implication of that decision would be an extension of my tenure in Aligarh. The home minister decided to bite the bullet and deal with me in a most polite and harmonious manner thereafter.

The year 1986 proved to be a very important one for me. I was blessed with a daughter who is one of the most precious treasures in my life. I had always hoped and prayed to have a daughter and the Almighty fulfilled my wishes. Daughters are always so caring and loving and without casting any aspersions on the tribe of sons, I think the adage 'daughters are daughters all your life; a son is a son till you get him a wife' is clearly well said.

On the official front, in February 1986 the gates of the Babri Masjid were ordered to be opened. Babri Masjid was a mosque in Ayodhya, at a site believed by Hindus to be the birthplace of the revered Hindu deity, Ram. The mosque, built circa 1527, at the command of the Mughal Emperor Babur, had been locked since 1949. It had been a focus of dispute between the Hindu and Muslim communities since the eighteenth century. The opening of the gates of the mosque had huge significance since it would allow worship of the Hindu deity by the followers of that faith. My DM called me to say, '*Naresh, Ram Lalla mukt ho gaye*' (Lord Ram is now free). Next, he asked me to come to the police headquarters. To be honest, the gravity of his message or his instructions did not sink in immediately.

I reached the police headquarters which looked like a war zone as we were told that the Muslim community in the city had come out in large numbers wearing black bands. The Hindus were rejoicing. The tension was palpable and felt most in the Aligarh Muslim University campus. We were on the brink of a major conflagration. With a great deal of deft handling, the situation was brought under control. The next five to six years would show what a major issue this became for the nation, impacting almost every facet of modern India's history and politics. We survived to live another day.

Aligarh constantly lived on the knife's edge. A relatively minor skirmish between the two communities over something as innocuous as an India–Pakistan cricket match had the potential to bring life to a standstill in the expectation of a major riot. I also deputised for the district magistrate whenever he went out of station. It kept me very close to both sides of administration, development as well as law and order. It was an amazing learning experience.

On 4 July 1988, late in the afternoon, I was suddenly called by the DM and told to proceed to Lucknow to meet the chief minister, Narayan Dutt Tiwari, who was popularly known as NDT, and had recently taken over. NDT was reputed to be a development guru. I got on to the first train, an overnight journey to Lucknow. I spent all night cramming the vital statistics of the district. I did not have a clue as to why I had been summoned by the CM. Could it be the home minister playing games again? I met the CM for all of two to three minutes. He gave me a long, piercing look as if to reassure himself that I was a normal human being, then shook my hands and simply said, 'Welcome!' I came back to Aligarh still clueless. Within three hours of my return, a crash telegram came from Lucknow. My DM handed it over to me. Transfer for sure, to some innocuous place, I thought. The home minister had succeeded. I opened the telegram and almost fell off my chair; I had been posted as a joint secretary in the office of the chief minister with orders to join within forty-eight hours.

The Chief Minister's Office, August 1988–November 1989

The time had come to bid farewell to Aligarh. The last few days of my tenure were hectic but in a pleasant way. I was at the receiving end of a series of farewell parties, which involved multiple lunches and dinners, including breakfasts and evening teas. The most memorable send-off though took place at the Aligarh railway station as I prepared to board the night train from Aligarh to Lucknow with Anjali and our two-year-old daughter.

Arriving at the station, I was astonished to see over 300 people, armed with marigold garlands and rosebuds, gathered to see me off. The platform was full of people, chanting slogans, idolising me. The crowd stalled the departure of the train, much to the chagrin of the other passengers. As I struggled to board, my 300-odd friends began decorating the train with the marigold garlands. My daughter, Urvashi, was horrified at the prevailing chaos and confusion. She began to scream at the top of her voice, making vain attempts—safe in the arms of her mother—to protect me from this friendly but unruly mob.

As the train started to move, the chanting continued as did the thrusting of rose petals my way. Some even latched on to my hands as I bid goodbye to Aligarh. The train had been delayed by over half an hour. As I entered my cabin, located in a second-class, air-conditioned coach, I found some disgruntled co-passengers. I occupied my berth quietly. An animated conversation was going on. They had quickly come to an obvious conclusion that some politician must be the cause of this chaos. The conversation veered towards how modern-day politicians had wrecked this country. I listened and having sensed that they did not associate me as the cause of this chaos, I decided to become an active participant in the conversation. Just then, a couple of my colleagues who had overzealously decided to see me off to Lucknow showed up and revealed my identity.

It was late and I decided to call it a day. While tossing

and turning in a rather uncomfortable berth, I mulled over my three-year tenure in Aligarh, in particular, the last ten days. It was full of nostalgia, self-satisfaction and a sense of déjà vu fuelled by elaborate farewell parties and long speeches eulogising me—all capped by the grand send-off. For a moment, I actually began to feel as if I were a budding politician. A strange nexus exists between politicians and civil servants in India, both finding the grass greener on the other side. It took me a few years to understand that the events of the last ten days in Aligarh had less to do with me and more to do with the position that I was going to occupy. A lesson well learnt: keep a level head and do not get carried away by flattery and false praise.

The next day, I reported at the office of the chief minister of Uttar Pradesh, the chief executive of India's largest state, home to over a 120 million people. At the time, this was politically the most important state, sending eighty-five representatives out of a total of 540-odd MPs. The chief minister of Uttar Pradesh wielded immense clout, as the prime minister, as well as several members of the Union cabinet, belonged to the state. However, by July 1988, the political landscape of the country had begun to alter rather dramatically.

The Rajiv Gandhi government, which had swept into power with an overwhelming majority in December 1984, was on a shaky wicket with one of his closest confidants and cabinet minister for finance and defence, V.P. Singh, having resigned and created a new political formation, the Janata Dal. National elections were due in December 1989 and Rajiv

Gandhi wanted a trusted, reliable and astute politician to head the government in Uttar Pradesh. Who could be better than the tried and tested Narayan Dutt Tiwari?

NDT had already served as the chief minister of Uttar Pradesh for two tenures and had held almost every major portfolio in Delhi, ranging from industry and commerce to external affairs. He was famous for his administrative acumen. NDT was also considered a visionary and was credited with having conceptualised the establishment of two major industrial townships, NOIDA and Greater NOIDA, on the periphery of the national capital of Delhi. I was indeed excited at the prospect of working with someone of such high stature. But soon I was to realise that my real boss would be someone else.

My boss happened to be the principal secretary to the chief minister, S.A.T. Rizvi, a senior and dignified man but a tough taskmaster. I did not have a single day's experience of working in the secretariat nor with government files. I was also not adept at drafting in administrative Hindi, which is very different from the spoken version of the language. I had picked up spoken Hindi in Aligarh and was quite used to giving speeches but written Hindi was a different ballgame altogether. My St. Columba's and St. Stephen's educational background was proving to be a handicap and rather embarrassing.

The principal secretary lost no time in explaining my role, which was basically to study all the files that came into the

CM's office and put up a 'dummy note' on each file. A 'dummy note' was a relatively new concept. It entailed an executive summary of the file, key recommendations and any advice that the principal secretary may have to offer. These 'dummy notes' would be seen and cross-checked by the principal secretary before its onward transmission to the chief minister. The concept of 'dummy notes' was borrowed from a practice that Rajiv Gandhi had introduced in the PMO. It was an efficient way to get files cleared, as the chief minister had instructed that all files received in the CMO by 3 p.m. of each day should mandatorily be put up to him the same evening. On average, I received fifty-plus files a day. Reviewing each file, assimilating the key issues and summarising was no easy task. It required precision and exactitude. I now understood the emphasis in the Civil Service examinations on word limits for answers. Preparing these 'dummy notes' was a rather painful task.

The principal secretary kept rather odd hours. He would come in late and take a long lunch break. His working day (or rather night) would begin at 6 in the evening. I would normally get an audience with him at 9 p.m. when he would go through each file and the 'dummy notes' that I had prepared. The scrutiny was meticulous, before he would sign-off the 'dummy note' for its onward submission to the chief minister. This daily exercise would go well past midnight, with a short break for my boss's dinner in the office. I was able to partake in the dinner which comprised delicious food, including kebabs and biryanis. I would reach home well past midnight. Urvashi would be fast asleep but Anjali would wait for me for dinner.

In a sense, I hardly got to see my daughter as she would leave for school early in the morning and I would still be asleep. Also, in the CMO, there was no concept of weekend or holidays. We literally worked twenty-four/seven, twelve to fourteen hours a day. I would have liked to spend some more time with Urvashi in the formative years of her life. One day she asked me why I kept such unusual hours and I found the easy way out and blamed my boss.

Anjali and I decided to nickname my boss 'Ceausescu' after the Romanian dictator who was facing a major revolt in his country before being executed by a firing squad in December 1989. Little did we know that at our next meeting with my boss, Urvashi would not only refer to him as 'Ceausescu Uncle' but even present him with a horrific caricature. However, it would be unfair to leave the narrative at this. My boss was a really kindhearted and affectionate gentleman, extremely competent and diligent, who could very clearly delineate his roles in an official and personal capacity. I learnt a lot from him. When I look back, as much as I hated my daily routine during those days, I was taught, step-by step, the art of precise drafting and the ropes of how a government works.

It was an invaluable experience for me to receive guidance from such a distinguished civil servant. I have cherished this throughout my career. I received true insight into, as well as a bird's-eye view of, the working of a massive state such as Uttar Pradesh. This would hold me in good stead when, years later, I found myself in a similar capacity—as the chief of staff in the office of the chief executive of an important and ticklish Geneva-based United Nations (UN) for over eleven years.

My encounters with NDT were few and far between. I accompanied him on a few occasions to his home constituency of Nainital and Haldwani, located in the Kumaon region, now part of the state of Uttarakhand. He was passionate about his constituency and it was amazing to see how he could identify each village as we flew over them in a helicopter. NDT's focus was primarily on development, a reputation he retained and that was best confirmed by the future prime minister Dr Manmohan Singh, who told me, 'You are lucky to work and learn with someone I consider the "guru" of development in India.' But that was years later and in another context.

On one of the trips to his constituency, NDT told me that his close confidant and cabinet colleague Gulab Singh, the tourism and culture minister, who belonged to the Garhwal region, now located in Uttarakhand, had been blessed with a grandson and that I should remind him to convey his congratulations on his return to Lucknow. This was sometime in end-August 1988 and I noted it down as one of the several routine instructions that one would receive from the chief minister. At that time, I had no inkling that this newborn would surface in my life twenty-six years later! I also accompanied NDT to Amethi on one occasion when Prime Minister Rajiv Gandhi was visiting. NDT introduced me to the PM and his wife, Sonia.

NDT's disposal of files was something modern-day politicians should emulate. All files sent to him as late as midnight would come back with detailed comments and his signatures by 9 the next morning. His queries were generally very searching ones, clearly indicating that he had scanned the files thoroughly. He had mastered the art of diagonal reading. It all worked like clockwork. The only solace and motivation I had when leaving my office past midnight was the lamp burning in the chief minister's office. NDT used to give all his instructions and approvals on the 'dummy notes', which I would transcribe on to the main files. This was always a cause of worry for me. What if someone were to challenge the instructions on the file as not being that of the chief minister. So, I religiously kept photocopies of all the 'dummy notes', nearly 10,000. I destroyed them twenty years later. In the litigious environment we live in, it is all the more important to guard one's interests while fully complying with the Official Secrets Act.

There was one interaction with NDT that I greatly cherish. I had created a computerised district profile of all the fifty-six districts of the state, a comprehensive document covering all the basic data, the list of ongoing projects, current problems and issues and the names of all the political representatives, including their political affiliations. A copy was presented to the chief minister the evening before his visit to a district in the state. He would normally read it on the way to his destination and arrive armed with all the latest information. It gave him an upper hand in all the discussions and meetings that followed. It was a simple but useful document and NDT was very pleased and gave me a pat on my back. I felt truly elated at this recognition.

NDT'S political sagacity was fully on display when Syed

Modi, an eight-time national badminton champion and a gold medallist at the 1982 Commonwealth Games, was assassinated on 28 July 1988. I was a few days into my job at the CMO and used to go to the K.D. Singh Babu Stadium for a quick swim after finishing my files and before my boss would arrive in the office for the evening session. The 28th of July 1988 was no different. As I was preparing to leave the stadium, I heard the sound of gunshots. I chose to ignore it as, sadly, this was not an uncommon occurrence in UP.

As I reached my office, the news about Syed Modi was flashing. The next day, Sanjay Singh, once a close friend of Rajiv Gandhi but recently turned political adversary, stormed into the CMO demanding that the chief minister declare a public holiday in memory of Syed Modi. NDT was in a meeting reviewing the implementation of drinking water projects in Amethi, Rajiv Gandhi's constituency. I was tasked with going into the meeting room and passing on the message from Sanjay Singh, who stood fuming and fretting in the chief minister's waiting room. I did as I was told. I went in and whispered the message in NDT's ears, who looked at me in a rather blank and vacant manner. I retreated.

Half an hour later, the pressure from Sanjay Singh was getting unbearable. I was ordered to go in again. The same sequence was repeated. I was really puzzled. Never had I seen a review meeting go on for so long. As the clock struck 1 p.m., NDT emerged, absolutely fresh and composed. His private secretary, K.C. Pant, told him about Sanjay Singh. I was also present. NDT went out to personally greet Sanjay Singh, who by that time was absolutely livid. NDT, in his inimitable style, held his hand and brought Sanjay Singh into his office and asked him to be seated. When he protested about his three-hour wait, NDT turned to me and said, 'Prasad-ji, why did you not inform me that Sanjay Singh was waiting for me? I would have left the review meeting.' I was shellshocked but decided caution was the better part of valour. NDT heard out Sanjay Singh and inquired from the chief secretary, who said it was too late to declare a public holiday. It was decided that a state plane would be provided to take Syed Modi's mortal remains to his hometown, Gorakhpur.

I left the meeting feeling totally nonplussed. Why had the CM not acknowledged that he had been informed? I came out of his office and asked K.C. Pant and he me gave two explanations, one of which I understood, the other will always remain a mystery to me. With a blank expression on his face, K.C. Pant told me that the chief minister would never like to declare a public holiday at the behest of an opposition leader and secondly that NDT was deaf in one ear. I blinked, wondering if I had spoken in the wrong ear, or if K.C. Pant was only trying to cover for his boss.

In another instance, NDT's political rival and adversary, his predecessor, Veer Bahadur Singh, then the Union minister for Communications, passed away in Paris in May 1989. NDT wanted his office to be represented at the funeral ceremony, which was to take place in Varanasi. The principal secretary and I were deputed to go and were offered to be flown to Varanasi in a small four-seater plane used to train pilots.

Oddly enough, the entry to the plane was via the wings and the cockpit.

The funeral ceremony was at the famous Manikarnika ghats of Varanasi, and attended by Prime Minister Rajiv Gandhi and most of his cabinet colleagues and many politicians. Night had fallen by the time we began our return journey. We were to land at the Amausi airport of Lucknow. Luck of the draw: our two pilots were trainees. One look at their faces and we knew that all was not well. The plane was circling the airport but our two crack-jack pilots could not locate the runway and it had become really dark by now. Just then one of the pilots turned back and gave us some chilling news.

The plane was running out of fuel. The fuel metre was going as stir crazy as us, dropping to the zero sign, picking up a bit and then dropping back to zero. My boss looked at me and said rather calmly, 'It's time to say our final prayers.' Meanwhile, the Amausi airport lights also went out. There was a power failure. Could it get any worse? All set for the end, we closed our eyes. Luckily, we then heard the quivering voice of one of the pilots: 'Sir, we can spot the runway lights now and we will attempt a landing.' The word 'attempt' was not very reassuring but after a tortuous two minutes, we landed, somewhat breathless but alive.

On the way back home, I asked my boss, 'Why were we sent to the funeral? Our presence was hardly noticed.' He smiled and said, 'Veer Bahadur Singh was seen as NDT's rival and in politics, optics count a great deal.' The next day newspaper reports carried a detailed version of the funeral with a one-line insertion that the chief minister's office was also represented at the funeral. For that one line in the newspapers, I had yet another near-death experience in the service of my country.

In November 1989, the Vishwa Hindu Parishad, a right-wing Hindu outfit, announced it would do a *shilanya*s or a foundation stone-laying ceremony of a temple dedicated to the revered Hindu deity Ram at Ayodhya, which they believed was his birthplace. On the same site, a mosque, the Babri Masjid, had been built during Mughal Emperor Babur's time. In February 1986, the gates of the mosque, locked since 1949, opened, permitting worship of the idols of Lord Ram which were placed inside the mosque. This had given a huge momentum to the movement to build a temple on this very site. While the permission for the *shilanya*s was given by the state government; it was also well understood that the structure of the mosque should not be damaged in any way. Suddenly, one evening my principal secretary informed me that the chief minister had asked us to go to the site of the ceremony and ascertain whether adequate measures were in place for the protection of the mosque. All this was to be done incognito, with pseudonyms and under the cover of darkness.

We set off late evening from Lucknow to Ayodhya, a distance of 135 kilometres which we traversed in an open jeep. We reached the disputed site late in the night. Posing as pilgrims, we offered prayers to the idols of Ram Lalla. We then embarked on a quick survey of the barricades and barriers that had been installed around the mosque. Our first impression was that these barriers would be good enough to regulate the crowd that may collect for the ceremony. We returned to Lucknow in the wee hours of the morning and submitted an all-clear report to the chief minister. Not even in our wildest dreams could we have imagined what was to happen at that very site three years later on 6 December 1992.

The CMO under the stewardship of NDT and the principal secretary worked in a very calm and sedate manner. I, for one, was totally insulated from the hurly-burly of politics. I began to enjoy this rather nameless, faceless identity because that is what civil servants are meant to be. Little did I know that in the same office, in the same capacity, I would find myself in a diametrically opposite situation. That is where I would come to understand the art of flexibility and adjustment in one's role as a civil servant. This is part and parcel of a civil servant's career and one word explains it all: agility. Agility in all its facets: situations, working conditions, milieu, bosses and more. The ability to adjust and adapt in a seamless and smooth manner is what differentiates success from failure. It is both a challenge as well as an opportunity to work in the Civil Service.

Chief Minister's Office: December 1989 to September 1990

In December 1989, state assembly elections were held in Uttar Pradesh along with the national elections. Rajiv Gandhi was replaced by V.P. Singh as prime minister. The Congress party, which had an overwhelming majority in Parliament with 404 seats, was reduced to a mere 197. The V.P. Singh-led Janata Party secured 143 seats. However, the most significant gain was made by the BJP which increased its tally from just two seats in 1984 to eighty-five. It was obvious that the electorate was confused but one message was clear. It was a mandate for a non-Congress government at the Centre. V.P. Singh announced the formation of a National Front with support from the most ideologically diverse group of parties, ranging from the left-wing communist parties to the right-wing BJP. The National Front had the makings of an unstable formation from its birth.

In Uttar Pradesh, the mandate was more decisive. The Janata Dal won 208 out of the 425 seats. Two significant markers emerged from these elections. The Congress, which had won 309 in 1980 and 269 in the 1985 assembly elections, saw its tally dwindle to just ninety-four in 1989. On the other hand, the tally of the BJP went up steadily from a mere eleven in 1980, sixteen in 1985 to a significant fifty-seven in 1989. Clearly, the political landscape in India's largest and politically most significant state was churning. This would have a huge impact on national politics during the next three decades.

The assembly elections threw up two victors—Mulayam Singh Yadav (MSY) of the Janata Party and Kalyan Singh (KS) of the BJP—both of whom would go on to be anointed as chief ministers of Uttar Pradesh. However, they had one more thing in common. Both would come to office on the crest of a wave and both would leave in controversial circumstances. I had never seen or met MSY, while I had worked and interacted closely with KS in Aligarh, where he was an MLA. In December 1989, MSY went on to become the chief minister of Uttar Pradesh. KS was the leader of the opposition.

The race for the post of the chief minister saw a bitter contest between MSY and Ajit Singh (AS), the son of former Prime Minister Chaudhary Charan Singh, who was a fiery and combative Jat leader belonging to western Uttar Pradesh. The contrast between MSY and AS could not have been starker. MSY was a grassroots leader with humble origins, while AS was an Indian Institute of Technology graduate, a master of science from the Illinois Institute of Technology, a computer scientist by profession and one of the first Indians to work for IBM. MSY was a dhoti-clad politician, AS an urbane technocrat. MSY had served as a minister in the Uttar Pradesh cabinet from 1977 to 1980, AS was V.P. Singh's industry minister in 1989-90. As the two became locked in a contest that took hours to settle, I hoped that AS would take over as the chief minister. There was one simple reason: my father-in-law, Amarnath Varma, had served as industry secretary with AS. I thought that would earn me an introduction to the chief minister. But it was not to be and the newly elected members of the legislative assembly opted for the firebrand MSY, a man I hardly knew, as their leader.

In the CMO the mood was sombre. A massive administrative reshuffle was expected to follow MSY's swearing-in. The axe would fall first on all officers working in the NDT CMO. We had been discreetly told to close shop and clear our tables. Strangely, I was feeling a bit relieved at the prospect of being freed from my morning-to-midnight routine. The swearing-in ceremony was held in the open and not in the governor's house as had been the usual practice. The principal secretary asked me to accompany him to the ceremony. On the way, he casually asked me if I had met the chief minister-designate. He looked surprised when I said no, since most senior officers in the state and all the officers working in the CMO had gone and paid their obeisance to MSY. We headed to MSY's residence on Vikramaditya Marg.

MSY was standing on the lawns of his bungalow, surrounded by slogan-chanting supporters, but for some reason he looked very tense. Outside, hundreds of cars with party flags were arranged in a cavalcade. All seemed set for the swearing-in. But then someone whispered to the principal secretary that there was a last-minute hitch. A final go-ahead was yet to be received from the prime minister. Apparently, AS had gone into a sulk and efforts were on to pacify him. In this very tense and chaotic environment, the principal secretary took me close to where MSY was standing, literally gave me a push and introduced me.

What happened next will always be etched in my memory.

MSY took out his hand, rubbed it on his silk kurta and shook my hand. Just then came the call from the prime minister. MSY rushed in to take the call. It was a green signal to go ahead with the swearing-in ceremony. Before anyone could realise, the chief minister-designate jumped into the nearest vehicle and was off to the venue.

At the venue, there were large crowds and a very festive mood. At the expected hour, NDT arrived, with all the paraphernalia of a chief minister, but who could have imagined that this was the last time the Congress would have its chief minister in Uttar Pradesh to date? In a simple but boisterous ceremony, MSY was sworn in.

The ceremony over, MSY, now chief minister of Uttar Pradesh, as per protocol, left first. NDT followed sans paraphernalia, very discreetly and almost unnoticed. I had a front-row seat to the change of power. It was exciting, amazing and in some ways harsh. Power changes hands in a split second. This is a great lesson for those in power: to remember that nothing lasts forever, least of all power, which is transient and temporary. The high and mighty of today could be dust tomorrow and conversely, people often rise from the ashes.

A colleague of mine and I continued to linger on. We were expecting the axe soon enough and so decided to stay back and enjoy some of the wonderful snacks being served in the VIP enclosure. Just then, a message came from the principal secretary, asking me to return to the office. I scrambled into my car and rushed to the secretariat annex, which housed the office of the chief minister. A specially designated lift took me to the fifth floor. Something looked very different that day. The lift, which was normally reserved for the chief minister and officers of the CMO, was packed to capacity with rather unknown entities. In fact, I had to struggle to get in and out of the lift.

I went to the office of the principal secretary. A normally calm man, he appeared totally hassled as he looked up and asked me to meet the chief minister. I complied. As I opened the door to the CM's office, I was shell-shocked. What used to be a very exclusive and well-maintained office was in total disarray. There were strangers milling around the room, some sprawled on the sofas and a few helping themselves to goodies from the well-stocked refrigerator—something unthinkable in the last regime.

As I made my way through this lot of people, I could not see the chief minister. I looked around and finally saw someone familiar: chief secretary Shiromani Sharma. He was shaking like a leaf. He pushed me towards an anteroom where sat the man: MSY. I went in, a small pink notebook in hand, and announced myself. MSY looked up and asked me to sit down. Here I was, facing probably the second-most important person in the country after the prime minister, with absolutely no support. All my seniors had decided to take a back seat. I sat down.

MSY seemed to be a man in a hurry, not someone who had a five-year mandate. He had probably read and understood the ground realities better. He gave me five clear instructions. First, there had been a train accident near Moradabad. MSY ordered that I contact the divisional railway manager and ensure relief efforts were undertaken immediately. The next three instructions pertained to NDT. I had to instruct the estates department that the house now allotted to NDT as leader of the opposition be renovated to perfection, that NDT be provided with adequate security and that he be given an extra car beyond his entitlement. The last instruction was the most telling. He asked me to go to the MLA hostel, gave me the room number of a very close compatriot who had lost the election and was sulking, and tasked me to pacify him and bring him to the secretariat. Having said that, he gave me his final instruction, that an informal meeting of the cabinet, comprising twelve ministers, be convened at 2 p.m. followed by a formal meeting at 5 p.m. As he left, he peered into my diary as if to make sure I had taken down all his instructions. There was an ulterior motive. He told me in no unclear terms that all work in the secretariat would henceforth be conducted in Hindi and that the use of English was prohibited. Next, he asked to be connected to NDT and in a flash he was off to call on the now former chief minister of Uttar Pradesh.

This five-minute interaction with MSY carried several messages. First, that he meant business and assumed responsibility from the get-go. Second, he displayed tremendous grace and magnanimity in his hour of victory over the vanquished. And, finally, he did not go overboard and gave his personal relationships utmost importance. For me personally, this five-minute interaction with MSY carried more weight and substance than the eighteen months I had spent in the CMO. It exposed me to a diametrically opposite way of functioning, one that was hands-on, direct and at times brusque. It showed MSY's connection with the masses and the common man. It rattled me and threw me out of my comfort zone. But it was an experience of a lifetime.

I quickly reported what had transpired to the principal secretary. Having done that, I headed to the MLA hostel. I tentatively knocked on door number six. No response. I knocked again and then again. The door opened slowly. Half ajar, a dishevelled and surly man looked out. I explained my mandate and sounded very important. This man from Auraiya simply looked back and told me to buzz off. What was I to tell the chief minister? After all, it was the first assignment given to me. I got a matter-of-fact response, 'Just tell him I'm too tired to come just now.' I thought to myself that he must be an important man and left alone.

Back at the Secretariat, I was almost immediately summoned by the chief minister. What was the outcome of my foray to the MLA hostel? he asked. I told him exactly what had happened, feeling almost guilty at not having been able to convince his compatriot. The CM sensed my discomfiture and smiled. He told me not to worry as he would himself go later in the evening to meet the man.

MSY moved with lightning speed on his very first day in office. The entire secretariat was agog and keen to get a glimpse of this man. He moved swiftly towards the cabinet room, through the corridor where my office was located, both sides of which were lined with the staff of the CMO to greet their new boss. And, lo and behold, he started to shake hands with each one of them before disappearing into the cabinet room.

The informal cabinet meeting ended at 4 p.m. and the first formal meeting of the cabinet was to follow at 5 p.m. A slew of electoral promises had to be fructified. The principal secretary was in the cabinet room and I was in my office. The arrangement was that he would keep me updated on the decisions taken and we would then prepare the press releases. Bank loans were waived off, promises of free electricity to farmers were announced, the procurement price of sugarcane was substantially raised. Basically, the message was clear: a pro-farmer and a pro-poor government had taken charge in Lucknow and the man at its helm meant business.

The cabinet meeting over, MSY went to meet his compatriot at the MLA hostel and was back in office around 10 p.m. With a simple, vegetarian homemade meal in front of him, he summoned the principal secretary with the list of officers serving in the CMO. The moment of reckoning had arrived. I began to pack my personal belongings from my office, a few photos and a couple of my daughter's paintings. Just past midnight, the principal secretary came back. He peeped through my office door. I sprang to my feet in anticipation. And, then came the news. MSY had sacked—or in bureaucratic terms, transferred—every single officer out of the CMO with the exception of the principal secretary and myself. I was tongue-tied. I did not know how to react. I could not imagine working in such an environment and adjusting to a totally different style of functioning from the NDT CMO—5 December had indeed been a long day. I went down the lift quietly, got into my personal Maruti 800 which I had bought to the office in anticipation of the axe and went home, totally exhausted.

The next nine months proved to be a totally different experience from the previous eighteen that I had spent in the CMO. Files and 'dummy notes' were no longer the priority. The chief minister was a leader of the masses and every action of his signalled a move in that direction. His day would begin at 8 in the morning with Janata Darshan, or a direct interaction with the people. Crowds of anywhere between 300 to 400 would collect each morning at the chief minister's official residence on Kalidas Marg while he continued to live in his old residence at Vikramaditya Marg. MSY had ordered a special enclosure for people coming from his constituency. He desired that the two joint secretaries, belonging to the IAS, be present when he went around meeting his constituents. Unexpectedly, he showed a distinct leaning towards IAS officers.

The next two hours would be spent going from person to person as he listened carefully to their requests. He would give orders on the spot, which we had to take note of for implementation. At the end of this exercise, he would leave and we would put all the papers that we had received from the public in a bag. Then, my colleague and I would order a sumptuous breakfast from the kitchen in the chief minister's house and, while it was being prepared, do some stretching exercises in the living room. Quite unthinkable today.

Loaded with papers we would head back to the office. After a quick consultation with the principal secretary, I would transcribe the chief minister's orders on each and every paper received. I took the additional precaution of entering the basic details into a computer in a simple format that helped me monitor the implementation of the orders. This paid rich dividends as the chief minister met public representatives in the evening on a regular basis and they would invariably raise matters that had not been implemented. I was present on these occasions as well. He tested me on a couple of occasions and the computer came to my rescue. Slowly, I sensed that MSY came to trust me as he asked me to take care of matters most dear to him. These related to his home district and constituency of Etawah.

In January 1990, the principal secretary was replaced by another very distinguished officer, Nripendra Mishra, though with a very different style of functioning. This required another adjustment. Two major changes in the course of a month were more than I had bargained for. But, in the Civil Service, one has absolutely no choice but to adjust and adapt and I learnt that very early in my career.

The chief minister indicated that he would like an IAS officer to accompany him on his tours of the state. I was asked to do so, in particular when he visited his constituency. MSY traversed the length and breadth of the state. These were primarily day-long visits with the exception of his constituency where he would generally spend the night.

On one occasion, the chief minister asked me to accompany him to Allahabad, where Prime Minister V.P. Singh was travelling for the first time after assuming office. The helicopters would take off from the open space outside the chief minister's official residence. Two cabinet ministers arrived just as I was to board the helicopter, seeking time with the chief minister. The pilot refused. I offered to back off but such was MSY's care and attention that he asked the pilot to arrange for another helicopter to take me to Allahabad. The chief minister took off. Then came the next helicopter but also another minister with a lady colleague. I again held back. Then came the third chopper and I took off for Allahabad, all excited at the prospect of at least seeing the prime minister. I landed safely and headed for the venue, the circuit house in Allahabad.

It was a chaotic scene with a huge number of people thronging the venue. Standing next to the PM, MSY signalled me to come closer. Then he gave me a chilling piece of news. The second helicopter had crashed. He said he was really relieved to see me. Having not yet recovered from that news, I got a huge blow in the form of a massive push from behind the temporary podium that had been set up for the PM to deliver a speech. Next, I found myself holding the prime minister of the country and trying to find my feet. The podium stabilised in a split second as the prime minister's personal security moved in. What an experience that was!

As for the helicopter that had crashed, we received news that it was hanging precariously on a tree a few kilometres away from Allahabad. Fire personnel brought the two occupants of the helicopter and the pilot safely down. The identity of the woman occupant remained a mystery as she had no official standing and it was thought best to bury the incident which had all the ingredients of a right royal scandal. Thankfully, this was in the pre-social media era.

During our various trips, MSY and I discussed several issues: the caste and class divide in India, the communal situation and how minorities required special protection, the lack of focus on farmers and the poor in government policies and schemes, and the neglect of the Hindi language. Politically, his archrivalry was with the Congress but that would dramatically change in a few months' time. I always found him to be a man of conviction and determination. His views were fairly rigid and obstinate. I tried to convince him about the utility of the English language and when he refused to budge, I asked him why he had opted for his son, Akhilesh, to study in an English-medium school. He looked angry at my query and turned away to survey the landscape that lay below us as we flew in the state plane.

As part of his Hindi promotion drive, he decided to visit the states of Andhra Pradesh and Tamil Nadu. Having served in Tamil Nadu, I was fully conscious of the sensitivity surrounding the imposition of Hindi. But MSY was adamant. Some Hindi scholar, purely for his own personal gains, had convinced him that the promotion of Hindi was entirely possible. He refused to see the futility of what he was going to do next.

Armed with a whole lot of promotional material, we headed to Hyderabad and Madras, the capital cities of Andhra Pradesh and Tamil Nadu respectively. We were housed in the Raj Bhavans or the residence of the governors of these states. It was sheer luxury. So far, so good, I thought.

The first stop was Hyderabad where a public meeting had been organised. It was a crowd of no more than 500 persons. MSY strayed from the path of promoting Hindi and launched a frontal attack on the president of the BJP, Lal Krishna Advani, who had recently announced his intention to traverse the length and breadth of the country in a *rath* or chariot, now famously known as the Rath Yatra, in the advocacy of a Ram temple at Ayodhya.

MSY's number one enemy had changed from the Congress to the BJP. As soon as he made anti-Advani comments, a hundred-odd protesters emerged out of nowhere, waving black flags. This was followed by shoes and chappals being hurled at the podium. One hit MSY. He was asked by the policemen on duty to leave. In the melee that followed, I ran behind the chief minister and jumped into a car. And who did I find sitting next to me? None other than MSY. He was in a rage and asked to be taken to the residence of the chief minister of Andhra Pradesh.

The state's chief minister happened to be Chenna Reddy, a baton-wielding, erratic individual who belonged to the Congress party. We drove into the chief minister's residence and as MSY went in, he told me that the minimum he would settle for would be the suspension of the police commissioner of Hyderabad. I decided to stay back with Reddy's private secretary, a fellow IAS officer. Two hours later, MSY emerged. I waited with bated breath for the outcome of this long meeting. I was told the local station house officer had been suspended for twenty-four hours.

The other highlight of our day-long stay in Hyderabad was a lunch with the charismatic N.T. Rama Rao, popularly known as NTR. A famous film star-turned-politician, NTR had been a very popular chief minister of Andhra Pradesh but was currently out of power. He served the most delicious meal with the best of Hyderabadi biryanis, *saalan,* kebabs but totally neglected the fact that his chief guest, MSY, was a hardcore vegetarian. While we all thoroughly enjoyed the food, MSY went hungry.

Our next destination was an even bigger catastrophe. In Madras, we were to meet the Dravida Munnetra Kazhagam stalwart, M. Karunanidhi, who was the chief minister. Before the meeting, I once again tried to convince MSY that it may not be a good idea to broach the topic of promoting Hindi in Tamil Nadu. But the Hindi scholar prevailed. He was even convinced that Karunanidhi had penned books in Hindi. So, off we went!

At Karunanidhi's residence, the chief secretary and I were to act as interpreters as both the chief ministers were determined to speak in their own languages, namely, Tamil and Hindi. I would translate MSY's words from Hindi to English, which the chief secretary would then translate into Tamil. And vice versa. What no one in the room knew was that I spoke and understood Tamil very well. The conversation started with MSY extending an invitation to Karunanidhi which was politely declined. Karunanidhi told the chief secretary to tell MSY that the last time he had gone to Uttar Pradesh, posters were put up all over Varanasi demonising him. The atmosphere was getting tense.

Just then, MSY asked me to convey to Karunanidhi his great appreciation for having written scholarly books in Hindi. I once again cautioned him but was rebuffed. This was really the last straw. Karunanidhi was visibly angry and used some rather unparliamentary words against MSY. I fully understood the import of what was being said but the chief secretary diluted its impact by saying that Karunanidhi had to leave for the state assembly. Basically, Karunanidhi had told us to buzz off. After this disastrous Hindi promotion tour, we returned to Lucknow empty-handed, with MSY trying to convince me that he saw a foreign hand in all of this.

My days in the CMO became increasingly hectic. I was on my feet from 8 in the morning to late evening. Most of the time was spent with the CM. I must admit I was getting carried away a bit with the high and mighty, including cabinet ministers, the chief secretary and senior representatives of the press and electronic media visiting me. I was beginning to feel far more important than my years in service. Then came some very sage advice from the principal secretary, who cautioned me against 'ballooning'. A very effective word given the circumstances. I wanted to follow his advice and slow down, but the CM would not allow that. I could see him getting more and more dependent and reliant on me. Normally a suspicious person by nature, the CM had developed trust and faith in me and the thin line between being a textbook civil servant and not was getting eroded.

My daughter was three years old and the entire burden of looking after her was on Anjali, who was posted as joint secretary in the industries department of the state government. I was located on the fifth floor of the secretariat annex and Anjali on the fourth. We attempted to coordinate and go home for lunch on most days and I looked forward to that break. If we were late, Urvashi would be back from school and this would usually be my only interaction with her besides an odd Sunday. One morning came Anjali's transfer order as chief development officer, Sitapur. It was a bolt from the blue! But the reason was far from routine. Anjali had blocked a crucial file pertaining to the appointment of an officer as the managing director of the State Mineral Development Corporation. The reasons for doing so were purely based on the Articles of Association. What seemed to be an innocuous issue flared up as the officer in question happened to be the husband of the appointments secretary, a powerful position and very close to the CM.

We discussed the matter and concluded that given my hectic working hours, it would be impossible for Anjali to move out of Lucknow with a child of three years. She represented to the appointments secretary. Expectedly, the representation was rejected. Next, Anjali sought an appointment with the chief secretary, a new and difficult character. He told her point-blank, 'Women who join the IAS should not marry and if they do, should not have children.' This was absurd.

I stomped into the CM's office and told him that Anjali would comply with the transfer orders, but in that case, my first priority would be to take care of my daughter. Consequently, I would follow a 10 a.m. to 5 p.m. schedule. MSY understood the gravity of the situation and immediately summoned the chief secretary. Then, something hilarious happened. I said I did not want to be present when he met the chief secretary. MSY looked at me with a winsome smile and asked me to stand behind the curtains of his office. I did as he told me and just in time as the chief secretary entered his office. MSY lost no time and minced no words but simply ordered the chief secretary to cancel Anjali's transfer orders. The chief secretary left, I emerged from the shadows, thanked the CM and left with a sense of pride. The next day Anjali was transferred to the Rural Development Department in Lucknow itself; the appointments secretary's husband became the managing director of the State Mineral Development Corporation; our family life remained intact and that was what mattered most to Anjali and me. But it wouldn't stay that way for long.

~

The decade of the 1990s was one of turmoil in the country, characterised by political instability, caste and communal conflagrations and economic distress. The National Front government in Delhi was already cracking under the weight of its own contradictions. The deputy prime minister, Devi Lal, resigned in March 1990. In August 1990, Prime Minister V.P. Singh announced the implementation of the Mandal Commission recommendations granting 27 per cent reservation to socially and educationally backward classes, or the OBCs, in government jobs and educational institutions. This led to violent protests across India. Meanwhile, the president of the BJP, Lal Krishna Advani, announced that he would embark on a Rath Yatra, a forty-five-day journey crisscrossing the length and breadth of the country to reach Ayodhya on 30 October 1990, to focus the nation's attention on the construction of a temple at the birthplace of Lord Ram. The resultant mix would find India in a conundrum like never before.

On the morning of 18 March 1990, my phone rang. It was a huge, black instrument, kept in the adjoining room. A landline. It was just 6 a.m. Who could that be? Anjali volunteered to answer. It was none other than MSY at the other end. A little hesitant he asked, "Is ain, ain there?" MSY referred to me as NN but pronounced it as 'ain'. Anjali was taken aback and rushed into our bedroom to tell me that the CM was on the line. I struggled to get out of bed, bleary-eyed, and picked up the receiver. MSY sounded a bit agitated. He said, 'They have thrown Devi Lal, the deputy PM, out,' and that he would like me to accompany him to Delhi. Realising that I sounded groggy, he said, '*Bas manjan kur lo, naha Dilli me liyo.*' Just brush your teeth; you can bathe in Delhi! Within minutes the CM's car arrived at my flat in Gulistan Colony and I left, totally confused as to why I was being taken to Delhi. I was worried on another account too.

When I reached the CM's residence, MSY was walking in the lawns. He got into the same car and we left for the airport. Once there, the first thing MSY did was to get me a cup of tea and a couple of buttered toasts. We landed in Delhi and I was dropped off at UP Niwas. I occupied a suite next to the one earmarked for the CM on the first floor. I got ready, had a hearty breakfast and switched on the television. It was full of news about the political repercussions of the deputy PM's resignation. MSY was being seen as a major player. But what was I doing here?

Lunchtime came and went but there was no sign of MSY. Then, worry began to grip me. I was going to Patna the next day on home leave to see my parents. It also happened to be my birthday. I simply had to get back to Lucknow that night. The last commercial flight from Delhi to Lucknow was at 7 p.m.

Having not received responses to several messages that I sent the CM's personal staff, at 5 p.m. I decided to take the plunge and see him myself. I was told he was in a high-level meeting in Haryana Bhawan. I sent in a slip stating my dilemma. Next, a messenger came rushing out, signalling the CM was calling me to the meeting room. I went in, little realising who was in there. The meeting was being chaired by the prime minister and present in the room were the chief ministers of Uttar Pradesh, MSY; Bihar, Lalu Prasad Yadav; Gujarat, Chimanbhai Patel; and Orissa, Biju Patnaik! I was taken aback. I missed a step and almost fell. I went to MSY to explain my predicament and all he said was that come what may, he would take me back to Lucknow in the state plane before my train left for Patna. I went back to UP Niwas and waited. Well past midnight, the call came that I should reach Delhi airport directly. MSY was waiting, very satisfied that the political crisis had been averted with the deputy PM withdrawing his resignation. It was a quiet journey back to Lucknow. Before taking leave, I asked MSY why I had been taken to Delhi. He said, 'I trust you.' That said it all.

In September 1990, I got a call from the appointments secretary that I had been transferred as district magistrate of Etawah, MSY's home district and constituency. The newspapers had already carried the news. Next, MSY called to tell me that a helicopter was ready to take me to Etawah and that I should join that very day. I resisted. I told him that this was not the posting of a police station house officer; it was a district and such transitions should be done carefully and gracefully. Besides, the district was not on fire. I told him that I would need to check with the DM, four years my senior, as to his convenience and only then determine a suitable joining date. MSY was clearly unhappy. He warned me that I would regret the delay. In retrospect, he was right.

My ten-month tenure in the CMO with MSY was in sharp contrast to the eighteen months I had spent in the NDT regime.

The style of functioning of the two chief ministers could not have been starker in their differences. NDT belonged to the grand old generation of politicians, very soft-spoken and polite. MSY was a firebrand who would not hesitate in calling a spade a spade. NDT had a formal relationship with the bureaucracy, typified by always referring to me as 'Prasad-ji'; MSY called me 'ain, ain'. NDT was a rule-book politician who understood and respected the line dividing politicians and civil servants; MSY demanded personal loyalty. Both could have become prime ministers of India—NDT in 1991, MSY in 1996. I consider it my good fortune to have been exposed to two such diverse models very early on in my career. After all, I was only thirty-one when I entered the CMO and thirty-three when I left for a posting as the district magistrate of the most important district in the state.

Etawah

I reached Etawah, a city on the banks of the Yamuna in western Uttar Pradesh, by train ten days later. A guard of honour was presented to me at the railway station. The senior superintendent of police (SSP) and the additional district magistrate (ADM) and several other officers were present to receive me. And guess who was the ADM—the swashbuckling Alfa! Fate would have it that our paths crossed again, working together but in very different roles. I was now his boss.

I got into my official car, an old-model Ambassador with a revolving blue light on the top. My personal security guard, armed with a carbine, sat in the front seat. I sensed I had just landed in very dangerous territory!

We reached the government guest house as my predecessor had not yet demitted charge and still occupied the official residence as well. As soon as we settled down to sip a cup of tea, news came that two people had been shot dead in the main marketplace of Etawah. The SSP, poker-faced, told me that this was the usual 'gun salute' when newly appointed district magistrates took charge. I thought to myself that this place was going to be quite a challenge. But some other hurdles were awaiting me.

I listened to a quick briefing from the key officials. I was fortunate to have three IAS officers working for me. Later on, we were joined by an IAS probationer, who happened to top his batch. This group turned out to be an extremely hardworking and committed team of officers. I had worked with Alfa and the city magistrate in Moradabad.

I looked forward to starting my stint in Etawah with great enthusiasm, keeping development at the forefront of my priorities. After all, it was the home district of the chief minister and the least the people of Etawah could expect was good, effective and clean governance. But very soon I became a victim of the circumstances well beyond my control. The priorities were going to rapidly change.

My very first challenge was to assume charge. Even though I had consulted with my predecessor regarding an appropriate date to do so, I met with resistance. He was reluctant to hand over charge. I went to the district magistrate's camp office but was told he was unavailable. This dilly-dallying went on for a couple of days. I wondered why and later found out. At that point, I wish I had heeded MSY's advice and joined earlier.

After a great deal of effort, I finally made it to the camp office located at the DM's residence and took charge. I entered an empty office. The house was still occupied by my predecessor. It was not the reception I had been expecting—it was cold and almost bordered on hostile. I looked at the board behind my desk and saw the list of all the illustrious officers who had worked as DMs in the past years.

I saw the name of Allan Octavian Hume, a member of the British Imperial Civil Service, who had served as an administrator in Etawah. He was in Etawah at the time of the 1857 revolt against British rule, often termed as the First War of Independence. Quick to understand that this was a revolt against the rampant misgovernance of the British, he tried to focus on development and establish Etawah as a role-model district. His outspoken temperament led to him being eased out of government service. In 1885, Hume became a co-founder of the Indian National Congress. I felt privileged to have my name transcribed on a board with Hume and several other luminaries. I clearly had big shoes to fill.

I took charge and occupied the camp office but not the official residence, which was shut off for me. I was told that my predecessor was clearing up but I would later understand that 'cleaning up' would be a better term. The less I say about this the better. In two weeks' time, I moved into my official residence, a palatial house with sprawling gardens and a forest as a backdrop. One would drive for half a kilometre, on a road flanked by beautiful trees, to arrive at the house. However, Anjali and Urvashi could not join me as my wife was posted in Lucknow and we did not want to disrupt Urvashi's schooling. I really missed them, lost in the huge house. Thankfully, Anjali and Urvashi would join me on most weekends and holidays. Having settled down, I began to get down to some serious business.

At this juncture, it would be important to understand the broader context in which I was working. In August 1990, the V.P. Singh government at the Centre had announced the implementation of the Mandal Commission recommendations. This had led to countrywide protests from those who preferred the status quo. In a countermove, Advani announced his Rath Yatra, starting on 15 September 1990, to Ayodhya.

The Rath Yatra would crisscross the length and breadth of the country, garnering support for the construction of a Ram temple at the disputed site where stood the Babri Masjid. Two chief ministers—Lalu Prasad Yadav of Bihar and MSY—were opposed to the Rath Yatra as well as the *kar seva,* which was to be performed at Ayodhya on 30 October. MSY made the famous statement, '*Wahan parinda par bhi nahi maar sakta*' (not even a bird can flutter at the disputed site).

The message to the administration was terse and firm. Do everything under your command to block *kar sevak*s from going to Ayodhya and protect the mosque at the disputed site without fail. Meanwhile, the Rath Yatra was having the desired effect. A frenzy was building up in the country in favour of constructing a Ram temple at Ayodhya. Slogans rent the air, '*Ram Lalla, hum aayenge, mandir wahin banayenge*' (Lord Ram, we will come and build the temple there). The battlelines were being clearly drawn; the hysteria increasingly shrill. Making matters more delicate, V.P. Singh required the support of the BJP for his government to survive, while his two most important compatriots, Lalu Prasad Yadav and MSY, were locked in a head-on confrontation with the BJP.

On 23 October 1990, Yadav arrested Advani and stalled his yatra. On the same day, the BJP withdrew support for the National Front government, which led to the ouster of V.P. Singh as prime minister on 7 November 1990. In retrospect, while Advani's arrest stopped the Rath Yatra, it aggravated the communal situation in the rest of the country with its epicentre being Uttar Pradesh. One such flashpoint developed in Etawah on 28 October 1990.

Uttar Pradesh was on fire in the days leading up to the *kar seva*. Communal clashes became the order of the day and most districts were under curfew. But it would be a shame if curfew was imposed in the chief minister's home district, I said to myself. It required massive effort to keep things under control. I would personally lead my officers on a round of Etawah city every evening and make sure that all the unruly elements were kept in check. The situation remained very tense but under control. This, however, was short-lived.

As the date of the *kar seva* came close, I was informed that several people were planning to march from Bhind district (in adjoining Madhya Pradesh, which was under BJP rule), through

Etawah, to Ayodhya. In my assessment, this would have been a disaster in terms of maintaining control of the law-and-order situation. First, Etawah was MSY's home district and he had by now come to be recognised as the primary roadblock to BJP's plans of carrying out a *kar seva* at Ayodhya. This even earned him the epithet 'Maulana Mulayam'. Second, Etawah city had a sizeable Muslim population. In the surcharged environment that prevailed in those days, my first duty was to maintain peace and tranquillity. I had to stop the *kar sevak*s from entering Etawah.

The districts of Bhind and Etawah are separated by the Chambal River, famous for its ravines, where lived some of India's most notorious bandits. A one-kilometre bridge over the Chambal connected the two districts, each state having jurisdiction over 500 metres each of the stretch. I consulted with my officers and we decided to erect a huge physical barrier in the form of a wall on our side of the bridge. All concerned, primarily, the Public Works Department, proceeded with building a formidable wall, 12 feet high and 12 feet broad, across the centre of the bridge, with brick, mortar, limestone and barbed wire. I thought it was truly invincible and my team got a massive pat on the back.

The divisional commissioner, Sumita Kandpal, inspected the site, as did senior officers from the state headquarters, Lucknow. Everyone was uniformly of the opinion that not a single *kar sevak* would be able to cross this barrier. We thought to ourselves that we were safe and 'mission save Etawah' was successful. However, not to take any chances, I called for the army to be deployed apart from several battalions of armed police. The army major arrived a day before the proposed march. I asked him to conduct a flag march in Etawah city, an exercise carried out in extreme circumstances, to display the might of the government and, in this case, as a warning to troublemakers. All seemed set for us to meet with strength and fortitude any situation that might arise. The extent of this miscalculation would be evident in less than twenty-four hours.

On D-Day, the SSP and I, along with almost every senior officer in the district, headed for the site which was a few kilometres from Etawah. The bridge and its surrounding area looked like a fortress. The wall looked like a majestic barrier. The SSP and I decided to take a vantage position and keep a close eye on the situation. Until noon, there was absolutely no movement from the other side of the bridge. It was unusually quiet. The one o'clock All India Radio news announced reports of widespread violence in various parts of UP with fifty-five out of its fifty-six districts under curfew. Etawah was the sole exception. The news reported that the situation on the Chambal bridge was quiet and under control. Everyone was going to be proven wrong in a few minutes.

My informants told me that in Bhind district, *kar sevak*s were going from temple to temple, with some prominent BJP leaders, whipping up a frenzy. They were being goaded to do a *kooch*, or invasion, of Etawah. I tried to reach my counterpart in Bhind but he was unavailable. I simply wanted to remind him that we should do our duty as civil servants and not get embroiled in the politics of what was happening. It should be our common endeavour to prevent an ugly situation and maintain peace. In several of our earlier conversations, he was in full agreement but on the day that it mattered most, he disappeared. One big disappointment.

Next, I learnt the army had unilaterally withdrawn without seeking my permission. This was a shock since the army, once it reports for duty to the civil administration, must act under its instructions. What the army had done was clearly unacceptable. Later on, I took up this matter with the army headquarters. The concerned major was sanctioned but, in his defence, he had said, 'I did not want to be part of a civil war.' Telling words to describe the situation. India had never been more divided than on this occasion—on the brink of a civil war between the majority and minority communities.

It was around 2 p.m. when we noticed a small crowd collecting at the other end of the bridge. Then, lo and behold, we saw a really emaciated and semi-nude sadhu striding like a lion on the bridge and heading towards the wall. A few hundred slogan-chanting people followed him. The most unbelievable sight that I have ever witnessed happened next. This frail sadhu climbed on to the railing of the bridge and within minutes he was on the Etawah side, past the wall. Had he fallen into the river he could have drowned or been devoured by the crocodiles the Chambal is famous for. But his spirit was indomitable. He stood firm, facing a district administration armed to its teeth, and said in a loud and shrill voice, 'Jai Shri Ram!'

As per tradition, the batch paid a courtesy call on the prime minister of India, Indira Gandhi

On the trek to Badrinath

With batchmate and dear friend Anil Swarup at Udaipur, on the Winter Study Tour

Course director Sunder Burra laughs sportingly at being mimicked

The journey begins: my first posting as an IAS officer

As chief development officer, Aligarh with my identification marks—the official vehicle and dafedar (orderly)

Aligarh, the top district in the PM's Twenty Point Programme: receiving the award from the minister in charge

Goodbye Aligarh: on the train to Lucknow—the affection and respect of the staff and people is the best recognition of one's work

Joint secretary, chief minister's office, Lucknow: at a function with Prime Minister Rajiv Gandhi, Sonia Gandhi and chief minister Narayan Dutt Tiwari

Consultation on matters of state with chief minister Mulayam Singh Yadav

As the district magistrate of Etawah

Getting a pat on the back from Prime Minister Chandra Shekhar on his visit to Etawah

Felicitating chief minister Rajnath Singh at a function as vice chairman of Kanpur Development Authority

With the chief minister of Uttarakhand, Narayan Dutt Tiwari, at the chief minister's residence, Dehradun

As tourism secretary, receiving the award for the top-performing state in the country in tourism, Uttarakhand, from the minister for Tourism, Renuka Chowdhury

Building India's intellectual property infrastructure: a modern office at Delhi

With Dr Murli Manohar Joshi, chairman, Parliamentary Committee on Industry, on his visit to the Delhi IP office

With director general of WIPO, Francis Gurry—a special bond formed during the course of our longstanding work association

With the secretary general of the United Nations, António Guterres

Called on the President of India Pranab Mukherjee to discuss various topics related to India's innovation ecosystem

Speaking at the 'Make in India' event organised by WIPO and the Government of India on the sidelines of the WIPO Assemblies of Member States

The International Yoga Day celebrations at WIPO, Geneva

With minister Piyush Goyal at the launch of the Global Innovation Index, 2019

With my daughter, the apple of my eye

With Bouncer, my companion and stress buster of eleven years

My family—my treasure, pleasure and support

'Jai Shri Ram' was the clarion call. Next, we saw the wall, which we had likened to the Great Wall of China, in terms of strength and solidity, come crashing down and a mob of 500-odd persons, fully armed and violent, triumphantly enter the Uttar Pradesh portion of the bridge. I stood there rather alone in the melee that ensued. Shockingly, most of the police force deployed on this occasion vanished from the scene almost as quickly as the wall came down. Hapless, I ran towards a posse of the Provincial Armed Constabulary (PAC), which was on reserve duty, and appealed to them to rise and save 'my dignity'. This personalised approach worked. Fifty-odd baton-wielding men sprang to their feet. Total mayhem followed. The crowd began to indulge in arson and stone-throwing and some bullets were fired. But as a result of the vigour with which these brave PAC men acted, the mob started to retreat.

Half an hour later, I missed a heartbeat at what I saw—the whole bridge littered with what appeared to be 'dead bodies'. I saw my career going for a six. Slowly but surely, these 'dead bodies' began to rise. It was late in the evening when peace returned to the scene, but leaving several injured and five dead. However, I had the satisfaction of not allowing a single unruly element to enter the district of Etawah. Etawah remained peaceful and my mission had succeeded despite my miscalculations on several counts, most of all the 'formidable' wall. Months later, I was given a state award for showing 'unusual courage and bravery in the face of adversity', which I dedicated to my entire team of loyal and hardworking deputies.

On 30 October 1990, the day announced for the *kar seva*

at Ayodhya, huge crowds gathered at the disputed site. Two brothers, later known as the 'Kothari brothers', climbed atop the disputed structure and hoisted a saffron flag atop the central dome of the mosque. The administration used brute force to dispel the crowds, leaving several dead, including the Kothari brothers, and many injured. However, MSY managed to keep the Babri Masjid standing, only partly damaged. Two years later, on 6 December, it was demolished. The chief minister on that occasion was not MSY but KS. No other event in the history of independent India has redefined the political landscape of the country as the demolition of the Babri Masjid.

After V.P. Singh's resignation, Chandra Shekhar broke away with sixty-four MPs and formed the Samajwadi Janata Party (SJP). With the outside support of the Congress, Chandra Shekhar was sworn in as the eighth prime minister of India.

In those days, political developments at the national level had a direct ramification in Uttar Pradesh. Reverberations of the split in the Janata Party were felt in Uttar Pradesh where the MSY government went into a minority. Like at the Centre, the Congress came to the rescue of the state government. The government of MSY survived, but only just. It would not last its full tenure of five years. Elections seemed to be looming large on the horizon.

In March 1990, the Congress withdrew support to both the National Front government and the SJP government in Uttar Pradesh. Chandra Shekhar resigned as prime minister and MSY as chief minister. Both were asked to continue in a caretaker role. General and state elections were announced for May–June 1991. The election in Etawah was announced for 20 May 1991.

The period between 30 October 1990 and May 1991 was tense and surcharged. The high-handedness of the state administration in dealing with the *kar sevaks* had created an atmosphere of anger as well as fear among the people. There was a clear sense of resentment. Specifically, three episodes come to my mind which were very representative of the mood of the people.

One day, in the midst of this situation prior to 30 October 1990, I received a call from the home department in Lucknow. A terse voice told me that Etawah district was not faring well on one specific parameter. I wondered what. Then it was spelled out. The district was lagging behind in the arrest of *kar sevaks* proceeding to Ayodhya. I was told that the district administration was duty-bound to check all trains traversing their jurisdictions, deboard *kar sevaks* and arrest them. I decided not to pay heed to this instruction. But it seems a similar message had been given to the SSP. That night, at almost 2 a.m., I received a frantic call on the twenty-four/seven helpline that I had set up. A packed train had been stopped at Etawah Railway Station, all the passengers had been offloaded and were being searched. A woman was crying inconsolably. She along with her children had been taken off the train and her luggage was being searched for tell-tale signs which identified *kar sevaks*, namely some food, pictures of Lord Ram and the proposed temple, a *kamandal*, or water pot, and a copy of the Ramcharit Manas. I rushed to the railway station.

The scene there was shocking. A train had been halted, every single passenger had been asked to disembark and their belongings were being searched by the police and railway authorities. The passengers were in a state of daze and confusion. I asked the SSP to stop this exercise and make sure that all the passengers were allowed to board the train so it could move on to its destination. God alone knows, the same treatment may have been meted out at the next station. While leaving, I told the officials who had indulged in this act to just place themselves and their families in the situation the passengers found themselves. I also said to myself that anyone who had been subjected to this ignominy would seek revenge through democratic means—their vote in the next election. And that is exactly what happened in mid-1991.

The second episode related to a cultural evening that the district administration organised in November 1990. This was a tradition and we thought it would be a good way to contribute towards restoring normalcy in the tense atmosphere that had been prevailing since 30 October 1990. Some of the most famous poets and *shayar*s were participating in this event. The turnout was impressive—more than 10,000. In order to avoid a larger congregation, we had installed loudspeakers at vantage points in the city for people to follow the event. All was going well when well past 1 a.m., one of the most popular poets went into a rendition titled *'Ramji ka Mandir banega dhoom dham se'* (the temple of Lord Ram will be built with a lot of pomp and show).

The audience joined the chorus which started to reach a

crescendo. It was getting louder and louder. The atmosphere was charged. Just then, I received a message that protest crowds had begun to collect in the Muslim-dominated localities. We were headed for a major flare-up. My first duty was to prevent a communal showdown. I had only one option. The poet had to be stopped. But to ask him to do so would have meant a huge and possibly violent reaction from the audience. My mind was racing. We did not have enough time. Then I whispered an idea to the SSP. Next, the electric connection at the venue was cut off. The crowds waited for nearly two hours, and after hurling a few abuses at the electricity department officials, they started to trickle out of the venue.

By dawn, everyone had left, disappointed, except for myself. Few knew or realised that we had avoided a major communal conflagration. After all, the first and foremost duty of any civil administration is to protect the lives of the people in their jurisdiction and to ensure peace and tranquillity. However, the conclusion that one could draw from this episode was that Etawah was on a knife's edge and would continue to be that way for several months to come.

The third episode was even more telling. In mid-November, I received a message that three policemen had been locked up in a room and set on fire. The incident was reported from Basrehar, a town with a population of around 10,000 people, twelve kilometres from Etawah. Along with the SSP and a strong contingent of police force, I headed there.

As our convoy reached Basrehar, there was lots of stone-pelting from the houses lined on both sides of the main street.

We headed straight for the spot where the policemen were locked up. There was a huge fire burning, mainly comprising vehicle tyres. A very foul smell emanated. Fortunately, we had brought a fire extinguishing vehicle and trained personnel with us. The immediate task was to extinguish the fire. Having done that, we broke the lock of the room where the policemen were held. They were in a state of complete collapse, gasping for breath, terror writ large on their face. We quickly got them out of the room, administered some first aid and sent them off in a police vehicle to a hospital in Etawah. But my job was far from over.

As district magistrate, it was not only my job to maintain peace and tranquillity but also to ensure that no one took the law into their own hands. I went back to the main street. The SSP and I got out of our cars and I ordered the police to enter the houses from where the stones had been thrown and bring out all the able-bodied men on to the street. Strict instructions were given not to touch the elderly, women and children. Twenty-odd men were pulled out of their homes, kicking and screaming. The trial had to be a summary one and the punishment exemplary. I asked them the reasons for their provocation. Instead of being apologetic, they appeared completely unrepentant.

At this point, I asked the policemen, already incensed by what had happened to their colleagues, to give them a thorough beating. The orders were executed with full vigour and perfection. Thereafter, all twenty of them were packed off to the jail in Etawah. However, this incident was yet another pointer regarding the disenchantment of the people with the establishment. The three policemen were only the symbols of that establishment. People would vent their feelings at the next elections which were looming large on the horizon.

The news reached MSY who was as caring about his constituency as a mother cares about her children. The people of Basrehar had given him a one-sided, heart-wrenching story about the excesses of the district administration. He called me and proposed a visit to Basrehar to apologise. I told him bluntly that this act would be tantamount to letting the district administration down and would not send a good message. Our conversation ended inconclusively.

Two weeks later, I received a message from the CMO that MSY would be addressing a rally at a place twenty kilometres beyond Basrehar. I was at the venue to receive him. However, I noticed something unusual. His helicopter dropped him and left. But his official programme mentioned that he would return to Lucknow after the rally. So, had his plans changed? Yes, indeed they had, as I realised soon.

The rally over, MSY announced that he would be going by road to Etawah. There was only one road from the venue to Etawah and that was via Basrehar. I decided to leave for Etawah straightaway. On the way, I crossed Basrehar and saw a huge crowd waiting for the chief minister. Later on, I got to know that MSY profusely apologised for the 'excesses' of the district administration but also cautioned the locals not to take the law into their own hands. There was one clear message in this whole episode for me—as civil servants we can rarely outwit or outdo our political masters. They will always find a way out.

The period between the fall of the V.P. Singh government and, later, the Chandra Shekhar government, in quick succession until the national and state elections in May 1991 remained a tense, difficult and complex one. The political landscape was unstable and chaotic. Socially, India sat on a tinderbox, beset with caste and communal conflicts.

The 20th of May 1991 was set as election day for both the sixty-six Etawah parliamentary constituencies as well as its six assembly segments. The assembly segments were home to the chief minister as well as two of his cabinet colleagues and were, therefore, considered not only VIP ones but extremely sensitive too.

In the run-up to the elections, the district administration worked relentlessly to ensure a smooth and fair election, with an emphasis on 'fair'—extensive touring of the constituency, hauling of antisocial elements, randomised deployment of poll parties through special computer software, provision of armed security to all the candidates. Everything in the rulebook was followed. MSY was pitted in his Jaswantnagar constituency against a notorious friend-turned-foe from the Congress and a reformed bandit from the BJP. It promised to be quite a contest.

I took the precaution of convening a meeting of all the candidates and their political representatives and read them the riot act in terms of dos and don'ts and the Election Commission of India guidelines. One of the guidelines forbade candidates from moving about on election day in large numbers. No assembly of more than five would be permitted, I insisted. Failure to comply with these guidelines would attract the severest penal provisions, including disqualification. Everyone seemed to agree. Events on the election day proved to be different.

On the morning of the election, I woke up at 4 a.m. and took a round of the most sensitive parts of the constituency, in particular Jaswantnagar. It was unusually quiet. My advice and arrangements were working. I reported to the central observer, a joint secretary in the Ministry of Finance, that all was fine.

At 7 a.m., I called on MSY, who had come the previous evening and was staying at the Irrigation Guest House in Etawah. I asked him not to leave the guesthouse with his supporters. To his query, 'How will I vote?' I assured him that a magistrate would escort him to his home village, Saifei, where he was listed as a voter. Having received an assurance from him that he would do exactly that, I headed towards Saifei, which I had anticipated would be a flashpoint.

The moment my convoy reached the outskirts of Saifei, a Basrehar kind of episode took place but with a twist. This time it was not only stone-pelting but bullets as well. A bullet hit my car. As this point, I stepped out. The firing was from the palatial house of the Congress candidate. I ordered the police to raid it. Holed up in the house, we found two dozen men armed to the teeth. Firearms, crude country-made bombs and other equipment were also recovered. Having brought this situation under control, I moved on to inspect some polling booths in the vicinity. At one of them, I found a large crowd outside while inside lay three dead polling staff. It is then that I encountered the most bizarre sight. Under one of the tables, I found a man shaking like a leaf. With folded hands he was begging to be spared as the crowd outside was baying for his life. It was none other than the Congress candidate! I pulled him out, put him in a jeep and asked a magistrate to take him to the safest place in the district: my house in Etawah.

MSY heard about the commotion and decided to break his deal with me. In retrospect, it was a natural thing to do. The chaos had been initiated by the Congress candidate but other parties, in particular supporters of the ruling party, were not to be left behind. Next, I found MSY, with hundreds of supporters in direct confrontation with the supporters of the Congress, who were all disguised as policemen on election day.

A fierce battle was on the cards. At that juncture, I went to MSY and reminded him that at that moment he was first a candidate and then the chief minister of the state. I told him with a straight face that I would arrest his supporters if they did not disperse. MSY got the message and he, along with his supporters, retreated.

The elections were marred by booth capturing, clashes, arson and violence. A dark day in the history of electoral politics in Etawah. For me personally, it was one of the worst days of my career, where I stood as a hapless victim of a political and electoral system beset with deficiencies. Fortunately, course correction would come in the years to follow.

I returned to the district headquarters well past 8 in the evening as poll parties began to arrive with the ballot boxes. Electronic voting machines had not yet been introduced in India. In all, a thousand polling parties would report to the district headquarters and submit their reports as well as deposit the ballot boxes which would be kept in a 'strong room', a secure and safe place, under lock and key, until counting day. Usually, the process of receiving poll parties is done by relatively junior officers of the district administration. However, given the mayhem that I had witnessed during the day, I decided to conduct these proceedings myself.

I went to the venue where the poll parties were expected. The first thing I did was to tell each poll party that they should not hesitate to let me know if there was any disruption in the smooth and seamless conduct of the elections or any suspicion of foul play. Expectedly, fifty of the 200 booths in MSY's Jaswantnagar constituency came in this category. The next worst affected were the constituencies of MSY's cabinet colleagues. In all, over 200 polling stations reported disruption. Armed with these facts, at 4 a.m., I dialled the Election Commission of India and requested to speak to the chief election commissioner, T.N. Seshan. I was literally walking into the tiger's den.

T.N. Seshan was a 1954 batch IAS officer, former cabinet secretary, recently appointed as the chief election commissioner of India, well-known as a firebrand and for his combative style of functioning. His one-point agenda was to cleanse the Indian electoral system and cast out the malaise that had crept in over forty years since Independence. In a loud, sonorous and irritable tone, he thundered on the phone, 'What makes you call me at this unearthly hour?' My voice quivering with nervousness, I told him in some detail about the happenings of the day. He softened a bit, then asked in a firm and authoritative tone, 'What are you recommending?' I said, 'Sir, this has not been a fair election. As returning officer of the Etawah parliamentary constituency, I recommend this election be countermanded.' Seshan was silent for a few seconds. Finally, he responded, 'So you are recommending countermanding the election of a constituency which returns the chief minister of Uttar Pradesh.' Quietly, I said, 'Yes, sir.' The call was disconnected.

It was 21 May 1991. I convened a meeting of my team to review what had gone wrong. Was it lack of understanding on our part, connivance of the local police, dereliction of duty by the polling parties or merely circumstances beyond the control of any district administration? It was time for deep introspection.

At 6 p.m., television channels flashed the news: the Election Commission of India, in an unprecedented move, had countermanded elections in five parliamentary constituencies—three in Uttar Pradesh, two in Bihar. Etawah was one of the five. This news sent shockwaves among the political circles and MSY's supporters were crestfallen.

Soon after, I got a call from MSY. He was calm but he was clearly making one last-ditch effort to retrieve the situation. He said I should go to Agra where a state plane would be waiting to bring me to Delhi. He had arranged for me to meet some powerful people in Delhi and work out a way to find a solution. I told him that as per the Election Commission of India guidelines, I was expected to stay put in the district unless he could get me a clearance and have it conveyed in writing to me by an authority no less than the chief secretary of the state. While signing off he said, 'For a politician, the loss of an election is a life-and-death issue, civil servants will never understand that.' Three hours later, I received written instructions from the chief secretary to proceed to Delhi for an 'important' meeting.

I had a quick dinner and left by road for Agra. It was a dark night. A violent storm had set in, with thunder and lightning, trees and electric poles uprooted, making my two-hour journey even more arduous. I reached the Agra civil airport where Ramgopal Yadav, a cousin of MSY and the think-tank for the SJP, was waiting for me. It was 2 a.m.

As soon as I alighted from the car, Ramgopal came out, literally from the shadows, as Agra airport was plunged in darkness, to inform me that the former prime minister of India, Rajiv Gandhi, had been assassinated at Sriperumbudur while on a visit to Tamil Nadu. The moment I heard this, I got into my car and left for Etawah. The memories of what happened in the aftermath of Indira Gandhi's assassination were still fresh in my mind. I had to be present in the district for any eventuality that may occur.

I reached Etawah at 4 a.m. and immediately convened a meeting of my team to work out the deployment of forces all over the district before dawn would break. It was now forty-eight hours without a wink, and the ordeal was not over.

The morning of 22 May 1991 was relatively quiet. The nation was shocked and outraged as Rajiv Gandhi had been assassinated by Tamil militants belonging to the dreaded terrorist outfit LTTE. Etawah remained peaceful but not the political circles. This time I received a call from the chief secretary to accompany him to Delhi. On my insistence, he sent me a written communication by fax. The plan was as follows: the chief secretary would come from Lucknow to Etawah, touch down, pick me up and fly to Delhi for that 'important' meeting that MSY had planned.

At noon sharp, the helicopter touched down at Parade Ground in Etawah. I jumped in and we were on our way to Delhi. Whilst circling over Delhi, I looked out to find the nation's capital totally deserted. Rajiv Gandhi's mortal remains were being flown into Delhi at the same time. An atmosphere of pall and gloom was evident at the airport. India was shocked at the assassination.

We alighted the helicopter and headed straight for UP Niwas where MSY and his key advisers were confabulating on the next steps. Apart from the Etawah elections, they now had to deal with what they assessed was a major vacuum in India's political landscape. I entered the room where my arrival was awaited with much anticipation. I was asked to explain the reasons for recommending the countermanding of the election.

I gave my reasons. Then a blunt question was posed.

Would I be able to change my position? The answer was an equally blunt 'No'. There being no room for negotiation, I was served a simple vegetarian meal and given leave to return to Etawah. While leaving, I heard an avid discussion on how state civil servants were more flexible than IAS officers, interspersed with the fallout of Rajiv Gandhi's assassination and the possibility of forming a third-front government at the Centre. I was dropped off by the chief secretary at Etawah just before it got dark. It was now sixty hours and I had not slept a wink. I came home, totally battered by the happenings of the last two days, collapsed in my bed only to get up the next morning at 10.

I was convinced that the election saga was behind me. I could now prepare to wind up and leave for Delhi on my next posting. I had received my orders for central deputation as deputy secretary in the Ministry of Commerce and Industry in March 1991 but the state government had asked me to stay back until the elections were over. I could not wait to leave Etawah. My nine-month tenure had proven to be a traumatic one, my role reduced to firefighting and maintaining peace at the cost of what I have always wanted, that is, development. However, what I did not foresee was another trying month ahead.

I was summoned by the Election Commission of India to appear before a panel headed by Seshan. What followed was not an 'appearance' but an inquest. At the first meeting, all the candidates of the Etawah parliamentary and assembly segments were invited—fifty-six in all, including MSY, his cabinet colleagues, candidates from the opposition Congress and BJP along with the key civil and police officers of Etawah district.

The session began with Seshan. He spoke out loud and clear and minced no words that all he wanted to hear was the truth and nothing but the truth. In a loud and thunderous tone, he looked at me and said, 'Now, the returning officer of the sixty-six Etawah parliamentary constituency will stand up and present his case.' Hopeful eyes turned towards me. Will I give a milder version, will I soften the blow? I stiffened. The moment of truth had arrived. The most defining moment of my career. I had to speak the truth and I had to speak with the same conviction and ferocity in which the question had been posed to me.

I spelt out threadbare the irregularities that had been committed on election day. With one sweep of my hand pointed towards all the fifty-six candidates, I said, 'They are equally to blame.' A hushed silence fell over the room. Even Seshan was taken aback. He then posed a simple but tricky question to me, 'In your opinion, what percentage of polling booths which report irregularities out of the total number of booths would justify a countermand?' My mind raced. In MSY's constituency it was twenty-five per cent, for the parliamentary constituency it was fifteen per cent. I said, loud and clear, 'Sir, ten per cent.' Seshan brought down the gavel. His decision to countermand the Etawah parliamentary elections was a correct one.

The decision came three days later, after we were all subjected to a gruelling interrogation. Seshan wanted to ensure that the district administration had been fair and impartial. It took quite an effort to convince him. All the paperwork that I had carefully maintained throughout the election process came in handy. While hearing my narration that I had come close to arresting the chief minister, Seshan said in a pompous voice, 'Even Seshan would have thought twice about that.' We were finally 'acquitted'. My honour was intact.

In all of this, the most telling memory that I have was a call from MSY. He told me, 'Even though your evidence at the Election Commission went against my own personal interests, I am proud of the fact that you spoke the truth.' How gracious and magnanimous of him. Not an iota of rancour or anger. My respect for MSY went up manifold.

I spent the next few days winding up to leave for Delhi. On one of those days, my executive officer at the Etawah municipality who fancied himself a palmist volunteered to read mine. All good things, as is usually the case with this tribe. Then he offered to answer any question that I would have. At that stage, the only thing that worried me was that I had never set foot outside India. I was the only one in my family who had not been abroad and I had turned thirty-four in March that year. He mulled for a moment and said with full confidence, 'You will go abroad on 1 November 1991 and you will spend half your career there.' I looked at him and smiled. Did he know the difference between the Indian Administrative Service and the Indian Foreign Service? I belonged to the first. Half my career abroad was ruled out. However, as my career unfolded, I learnt that he was right and I was wrong.

I left Etawah on 19 June 1991. It had been a tough nine months at the helm of the district administration. I learnt a lot and I was put to the test in a million ways. I survived but something about Etawah left a bitter taste in my mouth. I had no regrets about leaving and moving on to Delhi.

CHAPTER SEVEN

DELHI

On 21 June 1991, I took charge as deputy secretary in the Ministry of Industry and Commerce. On the same day, a Congress-led minority government, backed by the left parties, was sworn in with P.V. Narasimha Rao (PV) as the prime minister. PV was a veteran of the Congress party, having served in several important capacities ranging from home and defence to external affairs. In 1991, he had decided to retire from active public life but the assassination of Rajiv Gandhi brought him to the most important position in the country. He deftly managed to steer a minority government for the next five years.

Three days after taking charge, PV announced his choice of principal secretary to the prime minister. I heard the news on television: it was Amarnath Varma, my father-in-law. Most people who were expecting him to retire in June of that year were surprised but I was not. During one of my visits to

Delhi in April 1991, my father-in-law, a man of few words, took me into confidence. Rajiv Gandhi, who was on a hectic election campaign, had called him a few days earlier and told him that he sensed the Congress was returning to power. In that eventuality, Gandhi had offered to appoint him as the principal secretary. Gandhi had also signalled that he would like to embark on a process of economic liberalisation. Events took a different turn but it seemed that he had discussed this appointment with those who mattered.

I heard this news in Lucknow where Anjali and I had been summoned by the newly appointed chief minister of Uttar Pradesh, Kalyan Singh (KS), whom I knew from my Aligarh days. A BJP government had been installed in Lucknow, the party winning 221 of the 425 seats. MSY's party had suffered a crushing defeat.

We entered the chief minister's office to be very warmly received by KS. He looked up and expressed surprise that I had left the state on central deputation to Delhi. He reminded me of a conversation between us a couple of years ago, on a train ride—he to Aligarh and me to Delhi. He had said that if ever the BJP came to power, he would get me appointed as the DM of Aligarh. That was not possible now. As I took his leave, he smiled and said, 'A lot of people are baying for your blood, just because you were the DM in MSY's district, but I know your style of functioning, one which is totally fair and impartial.' The ones 'baying for my blood' were none other than my own service colleagues. This is and has always been the bane of the Civil Service in India: intrigue, the crab mentality and petty jealousies.

PV retained the industries portfolio. He used that as a launchpad to dismantle the Licence Raj as well as to introduce policies best described as the 3Ds: de-control, de-regulation and de-bureaucratisation. India was on the path of a massive economic transformation. This also put India on the path of globalisation. In 1991, it was more an imperative rather than a choice to rescue a bankrupt nation from economic collapse.

As a relatively low-level functionary in the Ministry of Industry and Commerce, I had no role in policy formulation. However, I did begin to sense how difficult a task it was to dismantle the old regime based on government licences and controls. I used to attend the Licencing Committee meetings headed by an officer of the rank of additional secretary. It used to go on for days with hundreds of applications being considered each day. The corridors of Udyog Bhawan, where the industry ministry was housed, appeared to be a fish market.

Representatives of companies whose cases were to be taken up would nervously walk up and down the corridors, breathlessly waiting for the good news that their requests for technology transfer, purchase of equipment from abroad or the terms and conditions of royalty payment had been approved. Something was not right. At least 'speed money' appeared to be the culture. In a matter of a couple of years, the work of this committee was at first diminished and then finally liquidated. Udyog Bhawan became far less busy. The reforms had started to show results. I was proud to be part of such a historical change, even though I was a very small cog in the wheel.

I slowly began to settle down at work. Delhi was a totally different ball game. The files required a great deal of attention as they could land up on the desk of the prime minister in his capacity as industry minister. I had to further perfect the art of drafting. Brevity was important. To differentiate the important from the not-so-important and the unimportant was essential. Senior officers had little time and even less patience to read long notes. So, basically, all key issues had to be in the first paragraph. Next, one thought to a paragraph. The first sentence had to contain what the ensuing paragraph would be about. The basic lessons of drafting were taught to me by some very patient and experienced seniors.

I picked up my official work in a couple of months but the real challenges lay elsewhere. In those days, it was next to impossible to get suitable government accommodation without a long wait. It took me over six months to find modest accommodation on Pandara Road. Next, we struggled to get Urvashi admitted to a school. It was an equally long wait before she could get admitted to Junior Modern School, close to our house. This school was not Anjali's first choice as she would have preferred her to go to Sardar Patel Vidyalaya, of which she was an alumnus and a topper in the school-leaving examination. Nevertheless, Urvashi excelled at Junior Modern School and was even appointed as the head girl. We felt very proud of her.

House and school settled, life in Delhi was calm and stable compared to what I had faced in the last couple of years, caught in the hurly-burly of Indian politics as a young administrator. I was, on most counts, very relieved.

Life in the central government meant a 9 a.m. to 6 p.m. job, generally free on weekends and some time to lead a decent private life. There were things which one had to adjust to, such as driving one's own car to office, eating home-cooked but cold food with office colleagues and basically learning to do things by oneself instead of being chaperoned by a dozen people all the time. In retrospect, it was great learning for me given my future assignments.

That said, one thing did bother me. I had still not stepped foot outside India. I applied for an Asian Productivity Organization-sponsored training programme, considered as very mediocre by Delhi standards in terms of allowances and perks. The programme was in Kuala Lumpur. I got all the clearances and was terribly excited. However, a week before its commencement, the programme was cancelled. It was a huge disappointment.

The 1st of November 1991 was fast approaching and the prediction by the executive officer of Etawah municipality was going to be proven false, I thought. On 30 October 1991, I was happily lunching with my colleagues, when a messenger came in and told me that the secretary wanted to see me. This was my first summons from the secretary, an officer of the 1956 batch. I froze but gathered my wits and walked into his room. He gave me a hard glare. 'What kind of proposal have you put up for your joint secretary's visit? How do you expect a joint secretary to be away for six weeks from the duty station?' he thundered. I stood quietly, head down. How do I tell him that the joint secretary, who was my boss, had engineered this trip from the United Nations Industrial Development Organization (UNIDO), a UN specialised agency, based in Vienna?

The secretary pushed his chair back, wrote something on the file and returned it to me. He asked me to hand over the file to the joint secretary. I did as I was told. The joint secretary opened the file with a smile at the prospect of a dream trip abroad. His jaw fell. The secretary had deleted the joint secretary's name and replaced it with mine.

On 1 November 1991, I was on the flight to Vienna. This visit, my first abroad, took me to Austria, France, the UK, Germany, Norway, Sweden, the USA and Japan. I traversed half the globe in six weeks. The executive officer of Etawah municipality had been proven right.

The next five years saw me travelling as often as six to eight times a year. I must have covered more than thirty countries. It gave me fantastic exposure as well as an insight into the ways of the world. A few episodes remain etched in my memory.

On one of my visits abroad, I was accompanying the Minister of Commerce and Industry who was set to deliver the keynote address at the general conference of UNIDO in Vienna. He was a senior politician who had taken over the portfolio from the prime minister. The official part of the visit went as planned. But something catastrophic was in store for us.

The Indian ambassador had organised a huge reception in honour of the minister and had invited a large number of guests from the Indian community, in particular from the state the minister belonged to. As we took the flight of steps to enter the palatial precincts of the ambassador's official residence, guests lined up on both sides of the foyer. The minister was accepting the greetings of the guests and looked very pleased. Just then, the ambassador introduced his wife. The minister folded his hands and thanked her for all the arrangements. However, the response he received shocked all those present and almost sent the minister reeling. She told him point-blank that it had been complete hell preparing for this visit, that his personal office had hounded her for the last fifteen days and that she was literally sick and tired. All this was conveyed in rather loud tones.

Indian ministers are not used to such a hostile reception, expecting to be treated as royalty. Setting that aside though, this kind of reception was totally contrary to Indian traditions where the 'guest is god' culture prevails. As a first reaction, the minister turned around, as if to leave the venue. We stood by, breathless. Fortunately, his political experience and sagacity came into play and he moved on to the main reception area as if nothing had happened. After things settled down a bit, I went and spoke to the hostess. She told me the details of how the minister's personnel had harangued her with requests ranging from tepid coconut water to delicacies from south Indian cuisine. Neither were easy to provide abroad in the early 1990s. I could see her point of view but protocols need to be respected. In this instance, the hostess had clearly crossed the line.

The dinner over, we headed back to the Intercontinental Hotel. The minister looked sullen but remained quiet. As we headed to our respective rooms, my secretary and I thought the worst was over. Thirty short minutes later, the phone rang. It was the minister's private secretary conveying a terse message, 'The minister would like to see you and the secretary.' It was close to midnight. He looked up as we entered the room and gave us a one-line instruction, 'This ambassador must be transferred out of Vienna before I reach New Delhi.'

The minister's flight was the next morning. We had all of twenty-four hours to implement the instruction. Unlike my old warhorse secretary, I was really perplexed. Two days later we were back to work when the secretary received another summons from the minister. This time he was more authoritative, bordering on angry. 'Has the ambassador in Vienna been transferred?' he thundered. The secretary left the room feeling less self-assured. He spoke to me and we drafted a letter to the attention of the foreign secretary. The letter was 'sent' but nothing transpired. Weeks went by. The secretary, sensing all was calm, checked with the foreign secretary. He was told that the letter was never received in the office of the foreign secretary. Luckily, time is the biggest healer and the minister never asked. An ugly incident was put to rest.

Another diplomatic incident occurred during a trip with my joint secretary for an Economic and Social Commission for Asia and the Pacific meeting in Bangkok. The meetings went well, we treated ourselves to some outstanding Thai food and looked forward to a dinner invitation at the Indian ambassador's residence. This is the usual protocol when senior officials from New Delhi go abroad. The evening started on a pleasant note. We briefed the ambassador on our meetings. Drinks accompanied by some succulent Indian snacks were served. There were about a dozen guests.

At a fairly late hour, the ambassador's wife invited us to the dining table. It was a sit-down dinner. We had barely begun to eat when the ambassador looked at his watch and became infuriated. He started to rave and rant, voicing his frustration at having to host these formal dinners every other night. Our hostess looked visibly embarrassed and in a hushed voice asked him to keep quiet. But that seemed to anger him even more. We stopped eating. It did not stop at that. The ambassador pushed his chair back and asked us to leave. We did as we were told to do. There was stunned silence in the room. We left, sensing that he had helped himself to one drink too many. As we sat in the car, the joint secretary and I burst out laughing. We didn't really have any other option!

Thankfully, these two episodes are the exception and not the rule. I had the opportunity of travelling to close to fifty countries and, without fail, in each one of these, the ambassadors and their team of officers were extremely generous and warm with their hospitality. I guess we need to understand the pressure on our colleagues serving in Indian missions abroad, of having to host social events virtually nonstop, making small talk, dealing with the idiosyncrasies of some visiting delegates. It requires a great deal of understanding on both sides. Our diplomatic service does a tremendous job of keeping India's flag flying across the world and projecting India as a nation with a rich history and culture.

Another memorable outing was a training programme organised by the United States Agency for International Development in Washington for a fortnight. It brought together thirty-odd participants from different parts of the world. It was an engaging training course, but what was more interesting was our after-work escapades. We moved together as a group, enjoying each other's company, eating and drinking into the wee hours of the morning. It was my first brush with living and working with the international community.

I was assigned the desk that looked after the leather industry among many other portfolios such as automobiles and UNIDO. It was exciting work. The leather industry in India had huge scope for modernisation and development. It was an export-oriented industry. The automobile sector, which was under licencing, with a monopoly of the Ambassador and Fiat cars, was opening up both in the four-wheeler and the two-wheeler segment. It was the largest contributor to the manufacturing sector in India.

The transformed landscape that we see in India today had its beginnings in the early 1990s. That is when Ford, Mercedes, BMW, Toyota and Hyundai, to name a few, started to plan to enter the Indian market. UNIDO provided me with an exposure to the world of multilateral meetings and negotiations. It was in these meetings that I learnt the ropes of the 'cut and thrust' of drafting in a multilateral forum. It was a unique experience which would prove to be immensely useful in my later assignments. I thoroughly enjoyed my work, which gave me fantastic exposure and insight into governance issues both at the national and international levels.

In association with UNIDO, I organised three investment and technology markets, initially called Intechmarts and later Invesmarts. The aim was to promote the flow of foreign investments and technology transfer to India. The first such event attracted investors from thirty-four countries and was a huge success. In all, 1,600 one-on-one meetings were organised. The venue was the prestigious Vigyan Bhawan in New Delhi and the event was inaugurated by the prime minister. The next two events were graced by the President of India. In short, these were very ambitious projects and were executed to perfection. As a consequence, several state governments, including Madhya Pradesh and Gujarat, went on to collaborate with UNIDO for similar events. Industry-specific events were also planned and implemented.

Another major event I organised was a Global Forum on Industry with ministers of industry of several countries in attendance. UNIDO had planned to hold this event in Bangkok. Owing to some disturbances in Bangkok, the event needed to be moved and the next choice was India, but there was a dilemma. The meeting could not be postponed. With only fifteen days left, the secretary received a call from the DG, UNIDO, with what seemed an impossible request to accept.

To make matters worse, I was laid up in bed with a terrible seasonal flu. I received a call from the secretary. I could barely raise my head and speak. Ten minutes later we signed off. The Global Industry Forum would be held in India. It seemed like an impossible feat but we managed to pull off a really successful event.

My five-year stint as deputy secretary/director in the Ministry of Commerce and Industry was a huge learning experience. It was completely different from what I had been doing in the preceding part of my career. The transition from the field to the state secretariat and then to the corridors of power in Delhi was at times a difficult and tedious one but I enjoyed every bit of the variety. In just fourteen years, I had the good fortune to work in two different states: Tamil Nadu and Uttar Pradesh and two different secretariats: the chief minister's office in Uttar Pradesh and the Ministry of Commerce and Industry in Delhi. I also benefited from fantastic exposure to international life, cultures, people and multilateral institutions. I could not have asked for more. After all, I was still only thirty-nine years old.

On the personal front, my stay in Delhi was memorable because Anjali, Urvashi and I were together. In addition, Anjali's parents and siblings, and my siblings were all in Delhi during these years. My parents would often come to Delhi and stay with us. We had several family get-togethers and spent really pleasant times with one another. In a family which had siblings in transferable jobs, it was a rare situation which I will always cherish as my best years. But this was going to get disrupted once again.

In March 1996, I received a direct offer from UNIDO to become regional coordinator, Investment and Technology Promotion, Asia-Pacific Region. It sounded really exciting and I decided to take the plunge in the unchartered waters of the multilateral world. My stint in Delhi had given me a sound grounding for such an assignment. I was to be proven wrong as the transition from a national civil servant to an international civil servant is altogether a different challenge, as I would encounter in the months ahead.

The first challenge was the separation from family. Anjali decided to take study leave for one year and accompany me. I was thrilled and the three of us landed up in Vienna. Soon after Urvashi's birthday, we received news that she had been appointed as the head girl of Junior Modern School. A third consideration was coming into play. We thought about it carefully and felt it would be unfair to deny Urvashi this opportunity. Anjali and Urvashi went back to Delhi. I was crestfallen but quickly learnt to adjust to the fact that as a family, in the future, we would have three careers to deal with and not one.

CHAPTER EIGHT

VIENNA

Anjali, Urvashi and I reached Vienna on 5 June 1996. Living abroad, rather than just a casual visit, was a totally new experience for us. I had to adapt to this new life devoid of lavish accommodation, chauffeur-driven cars and full-time household help like I had in field postings in India. Vienna would be different and the first challenge was finding suitable accommodation.

Fortunately, I had an affectionate cousin living in the Austrian capital and she insisted that we stay with her until we found an apartment, which we were able to do three weeks later. Like most Viennese, I used public transport throughout my stay. We had a house-helper from Sri Lanka assist us twice a week with cleaning and some other household chores. Cooking was entirely our responsibility. That was a real sea-change.

I joined as regional coordinator, Investment and Technology transfer, Asia-Pacific Region at UNIDO, located in the impressive Vienna International Center (VIC) with a nice office on the eleventh floor. My team consisted of eight people and I reported to the director and managing director.

The work atmosphere was entirely different to the ones I was used to. For starters, there were no bells on my desk to summon people, neither a red nor green light on my door. There were no paper files, most of the work was done electronically—completely different from India. There were no personal assistants to take dictations, but rather secretaries to assist with logistical issues.

The culture was also very different. Everyone referred to each other by their first names—no 'sirs' and 'madams'. In India, we generally work behind closed doors. Here, staff were expected to keep their doors open. As they say, old habits die hard and so I used to keep my door closed until one day there was a knock on my door and two women peeped in. I looked up, but before I could respond, they said in unison, 'So, you believe in a closed-door policy?' Having said that, but before even waiting for my response, they banged the door and vanished. My door always remained open after that.

On the work front, I struggled to create a role for myself. I convened a meeting of my team and quickly realised that each one was working in their silo and not as a team. There was no policy framework or guidance from the seniors. There was a complete vacuum in terms of substance, direction and supervision. I gathered that the functioning of international organisations, particularly the UN, was often individual-based and that supervisors found it difficult to instil a semblance of uniformity in approach or set common goals and targets. My first task would be to change this culture.

It was by no means easy. I had to really struggle with my peers and supervisors. What came naturally to me was unusual for them. I was summoned by the managing director and asked to fall in line. I resisted and requested that I be allowed to make a presentation to the larger group. With some reluctance, he agreed. I outlined what is akin to a workplan for my unit, with common goals and core strategies. It took a lot of convincing before I was given the go-ahead but I was warned about being held responsible should this approach boomerang.

After receiving the green light, I drew up a detailed workplan for boosting investment and technology transfer in countries of the Asia-Pacific region. India, China, Pakistan and the Philippines were some of the countries that would be covered under this plan. I took charge of India while my colleagues worked with counterparts in other countries. A very robust programme was drawn up and implementation began in earnest. It engaged the whole group and we started to work as a well-knit team. The results were impressive. We not only managed to get close to five million dollars into UNIDO's kitty but there was also an ever-increasing demand for our services. My team expanded; we became the talking point of the organisation. I became the favourite of the managing director who singled me out for an 'outstanding' rating in my professional evaluation. We were on a roll.

All this took about a year. Anjali and Urvashi came back from India and joined me for a year from 1997 to 1998.

Urvashi enrolled with the international school where, after initial hiccups, she excelled. One day she called from school to tell us that the children in her class had confronted her class teacher and questioned her about Urvashi securing the highest marks in English. The message was loud and clear: how can a student from India top the class in English? The class teacher brushed them aside and said, 'Look, she has topped not only in English but she has also topped the class!' Anjali and I enjoyed our lunches at the VIC restaurant on a regular basis. On weekends, we made trips to the iconic Prater amusement park, which Urvashi loved, and the world-famous Vienna Zoo, with its adorable pandas.

Soon, however, I was in for a rude shock on the work front. A deep-seated conspiracy was being hatched against me. A former secretary in India's Ministry of Commerce and Industry had joined UNIDO as the managing director. He became the kingpin in the conspiracy. The ambassador wanted his brother-in-law to get an assignment in UNIDO. A new appointment was next to impossible in UNIDO those days as the US, Canada and Australia had withdrawn from the organisation overnight, resulting in a thirty per cent cut in the budget. Several staff had been retrenched. So, the 'deal' was struck to get the ambassador's brother-in-law to replace me. This former secretary was well-connected in Delhi also. That made the 'deal' more secure.

My contract was coming up for renewal in June 1998. That's when I got a bolt from the blue—a final extension of just six months. How could a staff member whose record was considered 'outstanding' become redundant overnight? I just could not fathom it. I tried every recourse that was legally possible but met with no success. I was crestfallen at being the victim of a brutal and naked conspiracy. I packed my belongings and left UNIDO on 31 December 1998, sad and hurt. My colleagues were equally disappointed.

For months and years this episode left a scar on my psyche. I kept asking myself repeatedly how this had happened. After all, I was the one who had facilitated the former secretary's entry into UNIDO. Why had he been so vicious? Then, I suddenly remembered a statement he had made to me in passing. He held a grudge against my father-in-law on some score. Here, he got a wonderful opportunity to kill two birds with one stone—take revenge through me, and curry favour with the ambassador. I was only made a scapegoat for something I had nothing to do with. But, as I have learnt over the years, whatever is fated will happen. In such situations, it is best to bow in submission before fate rather than fight it.

I was destined to confront similar situations in the future but would be better prepared. Also, whatever God does, he does for the best. Had I continued in UNIDO, I would have had a rather mediocre career. I was destined for something better. As I look back, what seemed to be the end of the world at that stage turned out to be a minor scar, a jolt onto another path that led to the present.

I left Vienna a month later, bag and baggage, and reported to the authorities in Lucknow, Uttar Pradesh, for my next posting. A posting which would eventually turn out to be one full of challenges and achievements.

CHAPTER NINE

UTTAR PRADESH

The Sequel

Kanpur

Was it uncanny coincidence or fate that would somehow bring me back to work with the same people throughout my career? In Lucknow, I paid the chief minister, none other than KS, a courtesy call.

A BJP government was in power in Lucknow. I received a warm reception from KS who remarked that while Lucknow had developed, Kanpur, the largest city in the state, required a great deal of attention. He asked me to take over as the vice-chairman or CEO of the largest urban development body in Uttar Pradesh and, at that time, the fourth-largest urban authority in the country.

I had mixed feelings. On the one hand, I had hoped to take

over the industries department. On the other, I had always relished development-related work. However, I had no hands-on experience of urban development issues. This turned out to be my biggest blessing in the long run.

I took charge as vice-chairman of the Kanpur Development Authority (KDA) amidst great fanfare. My luxurious office was located in a huge office complex. The official residence was equally impressive. Clearly the best government bungalow in the city, it was spacious and very well appointed and surrounded by beautiful gardens. I was surprised by the retinue of personal staff at my disposal, ranging from cooks and gardeners to security staff (though I quickly reduced this contingent by half since I was alone with only weekend visits from Anjali and Urvashi, who had settled near Delhi). Air-conditioned cars, a generous expense account, personal security and every other conceivable frill to spoil an officer from day one were also part of the package. It was, indeed, a challenge not to fall for the bait.

Soon after I moved into the official residence, a short, portly, man introduced himself one day as its 'caretaker'. His duties were to take care of all the needs of the vice-chairman and his family. I didn't warm to the idea. It was feudal, not to mention repulsive. The duties of the caretaker were drastically reduced to taking care of the bungalow rather than of the vice-chairman or his family.

On my first day in office, I had four specific categories of visitors: public representatives, press and electronic media, stakeholders and members of my 1,200-strong staff. I was quick to realise that the job of the vice-chairman was going to be a tricky one as it was considered one of the most prestigious assignments in Kanpur and was constantly under public gaze and scrutiny.

The workday was fairly chaotic with visitors streaming in from morning to evening. The first thing I did was to streamline my meetings with the public representatives, the press and media, and the external stakeholders. I fixed two hours every morning to meet the public representatives and the external stakeholders. There were close to 1,00,000 external stakeholders—those who had bought land and real estate developed by KDA.

I earmarked one hour each day for an interaction with the press and electronic media. I did this because the most important newspapers and electronic channels had a representative specifically tasked with covering KDA, and I wanted to avoid creating a vacuum that would be filled by false and misleading news coverage or, in today's lingo, fake news. This strategy worked very well. On the one hand, I briefed the press and media about the key decisions that I had taken for the development of Kanpur city. On the other, I used this as an opportunity to educate them about key issues pertaining to urban development. This allowed me to establish a healthy and robust relationship with the press and media. The advantages were twofold. First, positive coverage for KDA. Second, the press came to my rescue in the battles that lay ahead with land mafias, corrupt builders and elements who were hell-bent on breaking every law under the sun. The press and media acted as my protectors rather than my detractors.

My staff comprised engineers, architects and managers. The engineering wing was headed by a chief with hundreds of engineers under his supervision. A chief architect was supported by surveyors, landscape architects and technical staff. Another major area was headed by the chief finance officer. I also had several administrative and managerial staff at my disposal. It was quite a handful to deal with, further complicated by a very strong staff union, infamous for its disruptive ways. They often called for a general strike or work-to-rule appeals on the most frivolous of issues.

So, it was a complex mix of public representatives, press and media, staff and the staff union, contractors and builders, external stakeholders and, at times, very difficult bosses.

The work of an urban development authority comprises regulating the building regulation law of the state and ensuring compliance with the masterplan of the city. In addition, it called for affirmative action in terms of repair, construction, including of roads, bridges and flyovers, and beautification, as required, of public infrastructure housing.

This charter of responsibilities had both a regulatory and developmental component. By its very definition, it would bring me into conflict with all those elements who were corrupt and did not wish to adhere to the law.

Kanpur was a highly congested city with several illegal constructions and encroachments. It was also rather filthy and unkempt. The responsibility for keeping the city neat and clean vested with the Kanpur Nagar Nigam, which was headed by a politically powerful mayor. But cleanliness was a necessary precondition for any beautification project that I would undertake. This would require developing an excellent relationship with the Kanpur Nagar Nigam as well as the mayor. Sadly, my experience was just the contrary.

I would also have to look after the interests of over a 1,00,000 stakeholders who had put in money to buy plots and houses from KDA and protect them from having to pay speed money and suffer other irregularities.

Next, I would have to deal with some highly corrupt builders whom I referred to as 'sharks' and who had broken most of the rules and regulations laid down in the Buildings Act.

I also had to contend with over 300 contractors who would undertake construction work on behalf of KDA. This would be no mean task considering how deeply entrenched they were within KDA as well as outside, with some powerful entities.

The staff and the staff union, in particular, would require deft handling. I would need to stem the rampant corruption within KDA and then motivate them to work as a strong and loyal team.

The press and electronic media would always require special attention and the relationship with this fraternity can best be described as walking a tightrope.

Finally, I had my bosses to deal with in Kanpur and Lucknow. The commissioner of Kanpur Division was the chairperson of KDA, while the principal secretary, housing, and the urban development minister in Lucknow were my supervisors.

Above all, I had to meet the expectations of the people of Kanpur who were waiting for the city to be cleaned, beautified and made more liveable. I was fortunate that my predecessor was a dynamic officer and had put several initiatives in place. I needed to take these initiatives forward, consolidate and strengthen them. A pretty challenging task.

I sensed my priorities would be twofold: one to plunge head-on into development-related work and the other to fight corruption. The first was going to be relatively easy, the latter not so much. As I had moved on in my service, my views and commitment towards fighting corruption had mutated. When I joined service, I held the idealistic view that I would fight corruption at every level. By this time in my career, I had reconciled to the fact that it would be good enough if I remained scrupulously honest myself and took the most severe action if I was aware of a dishonest act. I would move forward with these principles in Kanpur, with KDA reputed to be a den of corruption and rot. It was no easy task and my first confrontation was to come very soon.

I decided to set my house in order. This had to be done urgently. However, most importantly, I needed to understand how the mechanics of corruption worked. Why was the KDA reputed to be a corrupt organisation? I experienced the corruption the day I took charge as the vice-chairman. I was staying in a government guest house while my residence was being prepped for me to move in. After a hectic day, I heard a knock on my door late in the evening. I was surprised. Who would want to see me at this hour?

I opened the door to find a sleazy-looking man. He introduced himself as one of the major contractors undertaking construction works for KDA. With a rather straight face, he asked me about the 'cut' or commission I was expecting from contractors. I was stunned. I told him clearly that he was knocking on the wrong door, to which he responded, 'Yes, an officer's reputation precedes his arrival on a posting' and that my response did not surprise him. Unashamedly, he said he simply wanted to confirm. I spent a sleepless night.

This was the first time in my career that someone had the audacity to offer me illegal money. It went against everything I believed in. I knew the path ahead was going to be a difficult one. Unfortunately, this was not the worst of it—things were going to get even tougher.

A couple of days later, the chief engineer sought an appointment with me. I had already met him along with other senior officers. I was told he had an urgent request. I have always maintained an open-door policy for my colleagues. I have consistently believed in being accessible and have tried to cut the layers of bureaucracy that colleagues need to go through to meet senior officers. Having been a victim of 'personal staff dictatorship', I am totally averse to my secretary fixing my appointments. So, presuming it could be a health or a personal issue, I called the chief engineer. He requested to see me at my residence. I declined, impressing upon him that I do not see my staff at my residence for official purposes. He pursued, saying it was something 'personal' that he wanted to discuss. He had apparently read my mind. I relented.

Later the same evening, he arrived at my residence. Some pleasantries were exchanged. The conversation was progressing smoothly. It was about my earlier assignments, the development projects that were being implemented in Kanpur and a little bit about my family. I decided it was time to call it a day and quite discourteously got up and began to move towards the door. My body language was obvious. I was literally asking him to leave. Just then came the 'proposal' that he had been mulling in his mind. He asked me exactly what the contractor had done a few days ago. I was furious. I could not believe that such a senior official would stoop so low. I raised my voice and asked him to leave. He pleaded to be forgiven for this transgression and left. But this time it left me thinking. Was this the norm in development authorities? My faith in the system was deeply shaken.

The next day I convened a Town Hall meeting for all staff. This had never happened before. I clearly stated that I would not tolerate corruption. I made that statement little realising how deep-rooted corruption was in KDA. My first challenge stared me in the face. What would my strategy be?

I was told that the staff union and, in particular, its president, would be my main opponents in any fight against corruption. I had a long meeting with the president of the staff union and requested him to be my partner in my war on corruption. As a starter, I suggested we have a year-long 'moratorium' on corruption. It seemed to make a dent but I sensed I still had a long way to go. I would need to do something dramatic to win over the staff.

The festival of Holi was around the corner. My senior officers told me that it was a tradition for the vice-chairman to invite the senior staff and their families for a get-together at his official residence. I declined. The next day, I invited the president of the staff union to a meeting. I proposed that I would give a reception in my official residence and invite all the staff. His jaw fell. He could not believe what I was proposing. I told him to announce this to all staff. Come the day, I got the gates of my sprawling bungalow opened to each and every staff member of KDA. The reception stretched on for more than five hours. The scenes were touching as well as emotional. Some staff came to me in tears and said they had worked in KDA for decades, they had also heard about the vice-chairman's grand bungalow but never had the privilege of stepping foot into its precincts. It was a great feeling. A simple gesture on my part had given so much happiness to my staff.

The next day, the president of the staff union came to see me with a delegation representing the entire staff. They expressed their gratitude for opening my home to them and for my warm hospitality. I told them it was my duty, as the head of the authority, to act like a father figure. I told them that I always believed in treating my colleagues as my family. It was my conviction that one cannot treat colleagues as robots churning out files and proposals. It was far more productive to treat them like members of one large family. It is also my belief that respect and authority cannot be imposed—they must be earned. I was midway in the conversation when the stunning proposal came. The staff had taken a vow to eschew corruption. They wanted me to hold a Town Hall meeting and administer an oath to fight corruption in KDA. I could not believe what I was hearing. I looked more intently at the group in front of me. One set of the staff hierarchy was conspicuous by its absence—it was my senior management team. I now knew where the real problem lay.

The senior management team comprised a secretary, the chief engineer, the chief architect and town planner, and the chief finance officer. I referred to them as the 'gang of four'. It was a caucus difficult to deal with, let alone break. I spoke to them individually as well as collectively about my priorities. I explained to them at length the need to improve the image and credibility of the organisation. It seemed like water off a duck's back. In a few months, three of the 'gang' fell in line but the chief finance officer, widely recognised as the kingpin of the corrupt mafia, was another kettle of fish. I tightened the noose on all files and proposals that had a financial angle. But the chief finance officer always found innovative ways to get around my roadblocks. In exasperation, I requested for his transfer.

The principal secretary, housing, warned me about his political connections but I insisted that this officer be moved out if I was to function in a clean, effective and smooth manner. The headquarters relented. No sooner were the transfer orders issued than the chief finance officer, acting on a tip-off from Lucknow, proceeded on medical leave. In reality, he had gone to the Allahabad High Court to obtain a stay on his transfer order. By that evening, the high court had stayed the order and he had sent a pompous message to me through his supporters and well-wishers that he would come to the office the next day and start functioning as the chief finance officer. This was clearly unacceptable. In no way was I trying to disrespect the high court orders but the optics of this officer triumphantly returning to office would be a major dent in my fight against corruption.

I did two things. First, I decided to appeal the high court order in the Supreme Court. Second, I had to stop this officer from physically entering the KDA premises without attracting the contempt of court proceedings. I called the president of the staff union and shared my dilemma with him. His response was quick and fast. The staff would not let him enter the office the next morning. As I reached office, I was taken aback by what I saw. The majority of the KDA staff had blocked the entrance to the office. They let my car go inside. A few minutes later, the chief finance officer arrived, beaming and flashing the stay order from the high court. He was physically prevented from entering the office. Meanwhile, my appeal had been filed in the Supreme Court. By late afternoon, the Supreme Court stayed the orders of the high court. The staff went into a celebratory chant. I had achieved my purpose. The chief finance officer was out of KDA. The first major wicket had fallen.

With the staff backing me, the senior management team falling in line and the chief finance officer out of the way, it was the opportune moment for me to embark on a series of internal reforms. The first challenge would be to change the impression that KDA was a lethargic organisation, a den of corruption and one where exceptions were the rule. I insisted on punctuality. Leading by example, I would arrive to work at 10 a.m. sharp. That was the official starting time. Lunchbreaks were regulated to one hour. Lazing around in the sun beyond the core office hours was prohibited.

The human interface of the stakeholders with the staff, a major platform for corrupt practices, was drastically reduced. This was largely achieved through a massive programme of digitisation of records and contact through letters or emails. All the rights of the stakeholders were clearly displayed at vantage points in the office. Entry of visitors was regulated and only those with some genuine business reasons were allowed into the office.

I installed a glass door in my office so that I was visible to one and all. I encouraged other senior officers to do the same. Huge boards were put up, stating that this is a 'corruption-free office'. Some may question the efficacy of such boards or slogans but I firmly believe that they have a salutary effect. I also introduced a system of 'right to information' for stakeholders who wanted to view their files. They could also obtain a copy of their records. This hit at the root of the corrupt practices as very often staff would remove the payment receipts from the files, impose hefty late-payment penalties and then settle to restore the documents for something in return. Speed money was the order of the day. However, once timelines were clearly determined and displayed, this source also dried up. These were a few of the slew of measures that I introduced. This continued to be an iterative process throughout my tenure in KDA.

Having put the house in order, it was now time to turn my attention to the external environment. I had often heard that out of every rupee spent on a construction project executed by KDA, only twenty paise would actually be spent on the project. The rest would be frittered away in the form of a bribe, speed money and commissions. That was an astonishingly high figure. I simply could not fathom how this was possible and my senior management team would not give me a clue. So, I decided to go to the source.

I invited all the contractors on the rolls of KDA—over a hundred—to a meeting. I did not allow any officer of KDA into the meeting room though they tried coming in on some pretext or the other. I shut the doors of the large conference room. There I was, all by myself, facing a nervous and unsure lot of contractors. The first thing I did was to put them at ease. I said I did not know any of them but I had simply called them to help me understand where eighty per cent of government resources were going. There was a huge amount of hesitation to start with. No one wanted to speak. Finally, I said that I would delist them all if they did not tell me the truth. They began to sing.

It all started with the tendering process. I was told that the tender forms were handed out by the chief engineer to contractors who would offer him the largest cut. Then, the tender box would be kept in the room of the chief engineer, preventing a free submission of tenders. Thereafter, the assessment of the technical and financial bids would go through a protracted process, again involving money. After the grant of the contract, a certain percentage would be taken each time the next instalment of money needed to be released. Finally, to get the completion certificate done, more cash would have to be doled out. The beneficiaries ranged from the engineering wing to the senior management team to public representatives. I cannot generalise as there may have some exceptions but, according to the contractors, this was the rule.

The meeting over, I passed a few simple orders to cleanse the system. First, tender forms would be sold through banks. Second, the tender box would be placed in a public place, accessible to one and all. Third, I would chair the 'contracts committee' where tenders would be opened in the presence of all interested parties, including the contractors, and that contracts would be awarded on the spot. These meetings would take five to six hours to complete. However, after the first series of meetings, the association of contractors met me and thanked me for reducing the money they spent on commissions and bribes by twenty per cent.

The next challenge would be to stop the institutional commissions that were being paid to the engineering wing and the senior officers in KDA. I started a series of surprise inspections of all construction projects and made it mandatory for junior staff to visit each construction site as per a schedule. They had two choices: to release the next instalment if the work was satisfactory or record in writing the reasons for not doing so. I personally inspected all projects that were deemed completed. The contractors told me they had been saved of paying another forty per cent.

The last twenty per cent was the most difficult to tackle. These were monies given to the local body representatives who managed to be appointed to the major project boards. I decided to remove them from these boards as their presence served no purpose whatsoever except institutionalising corruption. There was a huge backlash against me on what they termed a draconian measure and an assault on democracy. Sometimes democracy proves to be a costly affair and this was one such example.

The contractors met me again, thrilled by these measures. It was now my turn to ask them a few blunt questions. 'So, how much of this eighty per cent goes into your pockets?' They looked down sheepishly and confessed that they were also a major beneficiary in this scheme of things. I told them point-blank that they had to put ninety per cent into the projects; ten per cent could be their profit. They agreed. This was a major breakthrough. *India Today* magazine reported on the Kanpur model and some other development authorities in the country began to emulate this system.

I had a deep sense of satisfaction regarding my early success with the anti-corruption initiatives. However, I had clearly stepped on the toes of several people, most of them powerful and influential. My journey ahead was going to be a sticky one with many battles to fight. Nevertheless, I decided to divert my attention to the development of Kanpur—a mandate given to me by the chief minister of the state.

It was 1999. India had just won the Kargil war with Pakistan decisively. The BJP, led by its charismatic leader Prime Minister Atal Bihari Vajpayee, was at the helm of affairs in Delhi. In the state, KS was the chief minister.

Atal-ji, during a visit to Kanpur, had famously remarked, 'Kanpur *kaisa abhaga shahar hai; jiske Motijheel mein jheel nahi; Ghantaghar mein ghanta nahin aur Phoolbagh mein phool nahin.*' (What an unlucky city Kanpur is—its three key landmarks, namely, the Motijheel, a famous water body, has no water; Phoolbagh, a historical site famous for its garden, has no garden; and the Ghantaghar, or the clock tower, was non-functional.) I decided to take this on as a challenge and develop all the three sites.

Motijheel, 600 metres in length, 105 metres in width and ten metres deep, was the site of what was once a lake. It was conveniently located just opposite my residence. I was told it used to be a beautiful water body, in a park famous for flowering trees. This was years ago, when the people of Kanpur would go to Motijheel for a leisurely outing with their families. It was also reputed to have been the venue where young couples proposed to each other. There was not a drop of water, nor a single light. What remained were broken walkways. The place used to be pitch-dark at night and had become a den for nefarious activities.

I quickly drew up a plan to clean the lake, which had not only dried up but had also been converted into a dump yard for garbage. The cleaning process revealed that along with the garbage were carcasses of animals. A hundred thousand truckloads of rubbish was removed from the bed of the lake. Having done that, we proceeded to get fresh water from the Ganga, on the banks of which the city of Kanpur was located. This was a complex process involving deep-bore pumps and pipes but was accomplished. I then decided to install two pumping sets within the lake which would serve as high-rise fountains. I was clearly borrowing an idea from the famous Jet d'Eau, the water fountain I had seen in Lake Leman during my visit to Geneva a few years earlier.

Having done that, we quickly developed the walkways, brought some flowering bougainvillea from Bengaluru and planted them around the lake, installed benches and chairs for visitors, opened a few kiosks serving snacks and cold drinks and built two impressive gates at the entrance to the lake, which I named Jai Jawan Jai Kisan, dedicated to the armed forces and the farmers of India. Boating was also permitted in the lake. On 15 August 1999, Motijheel was opened to the public in Kanpur. Within a period of six hours, more than 1,00,000 citizens visited the lake. It looked like a fairyland, with the fountain changing colours, dazzling lights all around the lake, ice cream vendors and balloon sellers having roaring business and, above all, families with kids and elders rushing to partake in the fun and merriment. Kanpur had truly been starved of fresh air and a clean environment.

My first major success, it drew accolades from what seemed like everyone—the people, the media—except the mayor of Kanpur city. She claimed that Motijheel was the property of the local body which she headed. She just could not swallow the speed with which this project had been executed and the unequivocal support and admiration it had received. KDA was on everyone's lips; the *nagar nigam*, or the municipality, which she headed, came in for huge criticism for its lethargic and corrupt ways. She headed to Lucknow to seek my transfer. She was accompanied by all the local body representatives whose 'commissions' I had stopped. But she did not succeed. The urban development minister, Lalji Tandon, and the government in Lucknow stood solidly behind me. This gave me the strength to proceed with my plans in a more concerted and determined manner.

Phoolbagh was called Queen's Park. During the reign of Queen Victoria, the then prince of Wales (later to be King Edward) had visited Kanpur in 1876. To commemorate this event, Phoolbagh was given the name Queen's Park. Later, after the death of King Edward, an impressive hall was built on the site and named the King Edward Memorial (KEM) Hall. The hall was used for cultural events and had a wooden dancing floor. The outer space was converted into a manicured and well-laid out garden. After independence, KEM Hall was renamed Gandhi Memorial and converted into a library. The garden was not maintained and the open space was used for political rallies.

I decided to embark on my next major initiative. This

was a relatively simple task. We employed the services of a landscape architect and recreated a lush and beautiful garden. There was one constraint, though. We had to leave enough space for political rallies. I could not convince the political parties to agree on this issue. I always felt this was a task half-finished. In later years, I was pleased to learn that political rallies were banned in Phoolbagh. At last, it has been restored to its pristine beauty.

My next task was to renovate the Ghantaghar and beautify its surroundings. This was going to be a tough job. Over the years, Ghantaghar, located next to Kanpur Central Railway Station, had become highly congested. It had also been converted into an unauthorised bus station, fully aided and abetted by the state transport department and the Uttar Pradesh State Road Transport Corporation (UPSRTC). A roundabout that existed in front of the Ghantaghar had been demolished and illegal hutments and kiosks had come up. The entire road leading to the Ghantaghar had been encroached upon. The area had become even more congested by siding built by the Railways close by. Over the years, the area around Ghantaghar had become famous for petty crime, drug peddling and the sale of spurious liquor. Ghantaghar itself was in need of urgent repairs and renovation. The biggest challenge was to make the 100-year clock, installed in the tower of Ghantaghar, chime and ring once again.

The repair work was undertaken immediately. A specialist was brought in from Delhi to set it right. This involved both art and science. Next, I negotiated with the Railways and bought a piece of land that was required for the beautification project. It was a long and cumbersome dialogue requiring several visits to Rail Bhawan to meet the chairman of the Railway Board. Removing illegal encroachments would be a difficult task. But by far the most tricky and cumbersome task was the one involving the government-operated bus station.

The encroachers on the road and around Ghantaghar were given notice to move away within fifteen days. Very few took these notices seriously. They were used to receiving them. Some money would pass hands and it would be business as usual. This time it was going to be different. I waited for the notice period to pass.

I had three situations to contend with: destroy the encroachments, shift the bus station to another site and develop the area around Ghantaghar. The development work was the easiest and began in earnest. Thereafter, KDA bought a piece of land from the Railways on the outskirts of the city at Jhakar Katti and converted it into a makeshift bus station. However, to shift the government-operated bus station would require the approval of the transport department of the state as well as UPSRTC. I tried my best but both were not forthcoming for weeks.

Finally, my impatience got the better of me and, in what turned out to be a rather rash act on my part, I summoned the demolition squad. We proceeded to the site which was buzzing with activity, as it was the day before Diwali. I waited for midnight when it would be quieter. At that stage,

I asked the demolition squad to raze to the ground every illegal structure in sight, including a government office of the transport department. The demolition was completed in two hours. I then asked all the buses parked in the area, nearly a hundred, to move to the makeshift bus station.

Suddenly, Ghantaghar and its surrounding area looked totally different and one leading Hindi daily remarked, '*Ghantaghar ne varshon baad khuli hawa mein saans li*' (the clocktower has been able to breathe after several years). Mission accomplished, I returned home at 3 a.m. and crashed. I was woken up at 7 a.m. with a call from the urban development minister. He congratulated me heartily. Then, he made a strange request. That I go to Ghantaghar. I wondered why.

On reaching Ghantaghar, I found hundreds of people celebrating and distributing sweetmeats. As soon as I got out of the car, I was mobbed by an ecstatic crowd chanting slogans of support and gratitude. It was a moment I would cherish all my life.

Later on, I received another call from the minister. This time, I was told that the chief minister, Rajnath Singh, would be coming for a *lok arpan* or 'dedication to the public' ceremony. We worked tirelessly to spruce up the area, beautify the roundabout, install sodium lights, widen the approach road and, above all, make the old clock chime.

The event was a grand success. The venue was overflowing with people. The chief minister was to speak from the rampart of the clocktower. The clock chimed 7 p.m. I was asked to be the master of ceremonies. Facing an audience, which, by conservative estimates, was 30,000 plus, was quite a challenging task but I survived. The chief minister stood up to speak and said in a loud and sonorous tone, 'I cannot believe this is the same old Ghantaghar of Kanpur; this looks like Marine Drive of Mumbai.' I was thrilled. What followed left me humbled. The chief minister continued, 'And the entire credit for this goes to one man and that is the vice-chairman of the Kanpur Development Authority, Shri Naresh Nandan Prasad-ji.' Though I celebrated for the moment, my sixth sense told me that this would mark the beginning of petty jealousies. I paid a heavy price in the months to come.

I moved on to even more important development projects, such as building a bypass road on a 'buy-operate-own-transfer' model, which was still a relatively new concept in those days. I also launched an infrastructure bond for Kanpur.

The infrastructure bond was intended to garner money to build twelve rail overbridges. One of the country's main rail lines, the Grand Trunk, passed through Kanpur. The city was criss-crossed by twelve manually operated railway crossings. This caused huge traffic congestions and an average loss of two to three working hours each day for most of the citizens in this city with over four million people. The only way to rid them of this hassle was to build rail overbridges. This was a costly proposition, requiring over fifty crore rupees.

Kanpur Development Authority did not have the money nor was the government willing to allocate such an amount. I thought it would be best if I could raise funds through an infrastructure bond. The first task was to get a decent rating from a credible agency. This required a great deal of paperwork but KDA managed an 'A' rating. Armed with this, I went looking for financiers. Most funding agencies were reluctant to invest in what was reputed to be a moribund and corrupt organisation. After stupendous efforts, I was able to convince ICICI Bank and Punjab National Bank to provide me the seed money.

I floated the idea to the public of Kanpur. The message was loud and clear. If they wanted development, they must contribute. It is not for the government to provide all the funds. This concept had worked very well for development of parks and green spaces in Kanpur, on the basis of a fifty-fifty funding mechanism—with both KDA and the beneficiaries contributing. People's participation and ownership is a critical concept in urban development, in terms of speedy implementation of projects as well as sustainability.

I received terrific response to both these proposals, but there would be several roadblocks. While I was busy with my development projects, my opponents were coalescing. This list of opponents included my boss, public representatives and all those who had a stake in the corrupt practices at KDA.

In fact, I had two bosses during my tenure. They were a study in contrast. One was a seasoned civil servant with many innovative ideas. He backed me to the hilt. The other one behaved like a Kanpur businessman who loved his drinks and dinners and was on friendly terms with private builders and developers.

During my entire tenure, I did not clear a single multistorey project as the proposals were non-compliant with the norms. To make matters worse, I regularly carried out demolition drives to eliminate violations to building and town planning norms. The builders had a friend in my boss. One night, after a day when I had carried out a major demolition drive in the city, my boss, who was by now not even on talking terms with me, called me to his home. There I saw him surrounded by those very builders whose properties I had demolished. There was plenty of liquor flowing. I was offered a drink, which I declined. Then my boss went on to reprimand me about what had happened that day. This was the last straw. It was an assault on my dignity and self-respect, something I would never compromise on. I stormed out of the room and told the government to either transfer me or my boss, as it was no longer possible to coexist. My boss was relieved of his responsibilities concerning KDA within fifteen days.

On the political front, the mayor, a couple of MLAs and councillors of local bodies, funded by the disenchanted builders, got together and decided to gherao the Vidhan Sabha in Lucknow. They paid a hundred-odd people to accompany them. They even organised a *rath* and a few buses to transport them from Kanpur to Lucknow, assembled in front of the state assembly and shouted slogans. There was only one demand: transfer N.N. Prasad. When I heard about this, I was not the least bit concerned. I pitied my detractors and felt an inexplicable sense of pride that I was considered such an important entity. Another message was loud and clear: my anti-corruption drive was working.

The Assembly episode had no impact whatsoever. The government's faith in me remained unshaken. I continued on the goodwill that I was able to generate among the common people of Kanpur.

On my journey from Kanpur to Dehradun, I reflected on my tenure in Uttar Pradesh. Kanpur was the last time I would work in India's politically most significant state. From 1985 to 2001, I had the honour and privilege to serve in Uttar Pradesh in some very difficult and challenging assignments. My thoughts were full of memories and images.

I cannot forget the first night that Anjali and I spent in an abandoned Awas Vikas guest house on arrival in Moradabad or the highly surcharged communal tensions that prevailed in that district. Aligarh proved to be an extension of Moradabad in this sense, but I thoroughly enjoyed the part of the work that focused on rural development.

The chief minister's office was a roller-coaster ride, working for two stalwarts of Indian politics—NDT and MSY—very different individuals with two very different styles of functioning and diverse ideologies. The episode between NDT and Sanjay Singh and my first day with MSY are the most enduring memories from my stint in the CMO.

Etawah was a different ball game altogether, a constant battle to keep one's wits together. I will never be able to erase the Chambal bridge episode from my mind. I would like to forget the elections in Etawah and the ensuing drama. Another scene that had a deep impact on my mind was the look of relief, almost joy, on the faces of some political leaders as they heard of Rajiv Gandhi's assassination. It was distasteful to say the least. It was also a poignant moment to see Sonia Gandhi seated on the floor of a train carrying her husband's ashes to Allahabad. NDT was accompanying her and as the train crossed Etawah he messaged me to arrange a Vicks inhaler apparently required by Sonia.

Kanpur saw my double-pronged strategy against corruption and supporting urban development take shape. Uttar Pradesh also had an excellent culture of 'service weeks' where all IAS officers of the state would gather for an annual meeting in Lucknow, both for business and fun. Organising a cultural event at the governor's house was one of the highlights of the service week and I was closely associated with that activity. I mimicked the high and mighty and wrote the scripts for a couple of skits, which were rather daring and bold. Something I would surely hesitate to do now.

I would be remiss if I did not mention some remarkable people who came into my life during my stint in Uttar Pradesh: my probationer in Etawah, a friend in Kanpur who is unfortunately no longer alive but his memory will remain with me forever; my bosses in the CMO; my first boss in

Kanpur and Moradabad, to mention a few. I also acquired my most endearing friend and companion in Kanpur, a Boxer who we named Bouncer. Bouncer was the only one to accompany me to Dehradun.

CHAPTER TEN

UTTARAKHAND

In 2001, Bouncer and I reached Dehradun on a bright and sunny spring morning. I put up at Anjali's aunts' homes, two of the most wonderful people I have ever met.

Uttarakhand was created on 9 November 2000, out of the state of Uttar Pradesh, following a people's movement that started in 1994 seeking a separate state. It comprised what is referred to in the ancient Hindu scriptures as Kedarkhand (Garhwal) and Manaskhand (Kumaon), crossed by the mighty Himalayan range of mountains in the north, with sixty-five per cent of its land mass being under forest cover.

Uttarakhand is also known as Devbhumi, the Land of Gods, and has some of Hinduism's most famous pilgrimage sites such as Badrinath and Kedarnath, Haridwar and Rishikesh, Gangotri and Yamnotri, and Hemkund Sahib, to name a few. Ashoka edicts from the second century BC at Kalsi point to the advent of Buddhism. Vyasa is said to have scripted the Hindu epic Mahabharata in Uttarakhand.

In terms of natural beauty, the state is pristine. Awesome mountains, including the second-highest peak in India, Nanda Devi at 7,816 metres; mighty rivers such as the Ganga and Yamuna have their source in the Gangotri and Yamnotri glaciers; and lush-green forests with world-famous wildlife parks such as the Jim Corbett Park, home to the famous Bengal Tiger. The Valley of Flowers, with the most exquisite species of plants and trees, recognised by UNESCO as a World Heritage site, is also located in Uttarakhand. Besides, famous national institutions such as Forest Research Institute and the Indian Military Academy, along with a host of other significant research and development bodies, also lie within the precincts of Uttarakhand. It is also a hub for school education and has several top-rated institutions. Lakes and hill stations adorn the state.

Unfortunately, over the years, the region did not receive the attention and importance it deserved. Geographically a long distance from the state capital of Uttar Pradesh, Lucknow, it suffered from gross neglect. It was almost considered as the Andamans of Uttar Pradesh where a posting to the hills was viewed as a punishment. It was against this backdrop that the people of the hill regions began a long and protracted battle for statehood. Quite naturally, the expectations of the people of the newly formed state were sky-high. They expected action and results-oriented development and all at supersonic speed.

Having served in Uttar Pradesh, coming to Uttarakhand seemed to be a comedown in more senses than one. Uttar Pradesh had a population of twelve crore; Uttarakhand merely one crore. For administrative purposes, Uttar Pradesh was divided into eighteen divisions and seventy-five districts; Uttarakhand had two divisions and thirteen districts. Having served in the office of the chief minister, district magistrate in Etawah and vice-chairman, KDA, Kanpur, Uttarakhand appeared to be a setback in my career. As I settled down to work, I realised how incorrect my perception was. Uttarakhand proved to be a very challenging and exciting part of my journey. But it was still a while before I would settle down.

On the personal front, I moved into a well-settled establishment and was really taken care of by Anjali's aunts. I was totally pampered. The challenge was on the official front.

I reached the Bijapur guesthouse where my batchmate, who was the appointments secretary, had asked me to see him. He was not present and I was told that he would arrive in a couple of hours. I waited for much longer and enquired once again about his whereabouts. I was tersely told that when I hear the drone of the helicopter, I should presume he was about to arrive. Apparently, the state helicopter was liberally used by officers to conduct their travel. I was impressed.

I heard the drone sound. My batchmate turned up at the guesthouse ten minutes later. We exchanged warm greetings and then he handed me a list of departments where I would serve as secretary. I was shocked. It contained twenty-eight departments. One glance at the list made me understand that the ones listed were mostly innocuous. Given my lack of interest in serving in Uttarakhand, I didn't mind.

My next meeting was with the chief secretary. He was pleased that I had decided to move to Uttarakhand. He then asked the appointments secretary to give him my work distribution. He quickly glanced at the list of departments proposed to be allocated to me, flung the paper in a rather dismissive manner and asked me to accompany him to meet the chief minister. A BJP government was at the helm with Nityanand Swami as the chief minister. Swami sized me up as the chief secretary told him that he wanted me to look after the ministries of Tourism and Commerce and Industry, among others. In a split second, my work distribution had changed. I had landed up with the most prestigious departments since these two contributed significantly to the economy of Uttarakhand; both had immense possibilities and potential to develop and grow and posed the first major challenge for the newly created state to meet the aspirations of its people.

In addition, I was given charge of several other ministries, namely, Culture, Sports and Youth Affairs, Labour and Religious Affairs. I was made the chairperson of two government-run corporations, the Garhwal Mandal Vikas Nigam and the Kumaon Mandal Vikas Nigam. Later, I was made the secretary of the Ministry of Information and Public Relations. It was a major portfolio. But that was the least of it.

The real challenge lay in the human resources and the infrastructure available to us. We literally had to start from scratch. I was allotted a room in a dilapidated building of the Ministry of Labour. A table and chair were all I had. No one who looks at the plush offices of the Uttarakhand secretariat would ever believe these humble beginnings.

The first task was to recruit staff to assist me. I identified five to six and began to train them. A couple of them would sit in my room which the chief secretary termed the 'war zone'. We then went on to sort out files and papers which had come in truckloads from Uttar Pradesh. New files were created and numbered and arranged into proper shelves. I computerised all my files so that tracking them would be easier than navigating physical files.

The next challenge was to determine the administrative structure for each of the departments. Also, new policies had to be drawn up. We came up with the mining, tourism, industry and, later, sports policies. This was a tedious and time-consuming exercise. The chief secretary led the process and it was not unusual for him to convene meetings at 8 p.m. which could go well past midnight.

The administrative structures and policies determined that our next task was to quickly implement the approvals given to us by the state cabinet. This was not going to be easy, given the limited human and financial resources that we had at our disposal. It would be important to prioritise.

I set my eyes as tourism, industry and information. As I began to work on tourism, I quickly realised that it was a major charge. After a few months, I decided to shed industry. With the tourism policy in place, we embarked on an ambitious plan of putting Uttarakhand on the world map. The first task was to finalise a logo and a slogan. After a great deal of brainstorming, we settled on an attractive logo symbolising the rivers and forests, the mountains and, above all, the spirituality of Uttarakhand. On the slogan, we opted for 'Uttarakhand: Simply Heaven!'

Uttarakhand is perhaps one of the most beautiful geographical entities in the world. The sheer variety in its beauty and landscapes makes it a breathtaking destination for tourists. I often think it is a gross understatement to refer to Uttarakhand as the 'Switzerland of India'. Frankly speaking, it offers all that Switzerland has and much more.

The obvious question that came to mind then was: why wasn't Uttarakhand a global destination for tourists? Basically, for two reasons: lack of marketing and promotion and the absence of world-class infrastructure. I decided to concentrate my efforts on both fronts.

Regarding the marketing and promotion, our efforts were two-pronged. We targeted domestic tourists as well as foreigners. For promotion of domestic tourism, we organised Uttarakhand Festivals in different parts of the country, highlighting the key tourist destinations, the rich cultural heritage and the authentic cuisine of Uttarakhand. These were runaway successes. Visitors to these festivals booked packages offered by the state-run tourist corporations by the hundreds. However, domestic tourists did not contribute to the economy of the state in any significant way. In fact, some people were of the view that they impacted the environment adversely and, in the long run, were a drain on the state's natural resources and wealth. I had a different take. How could we keep a jewel away from fellow Indians? It was their right to partake in what God and nature had blessed the Devbhumi with.

In parallel, we embarked on a major promotional campaign abroad. Our main tools for doing so were coffee-table books, videos, an interactive website and participation in the world's two most important tourism meets: the World Tourism Market in London and the International Tourism Bourse in Berlin. Quite a few perceived this as being overambitious but my answer to them was that if you don't have big ideas, you simply remain in a rathole. The impact of these participations was overwhelming. Several foreign tour companies booked to visit Uttarakhand.

Addressing the lack of world-class infrastructure, I made Ananda, a world-class spa in Narendranagar, the centre of my campaign. Ananda, located in the Himalayas, housed partly in the palace of the maharaja of Tehri, had an outstanding spa and overlooked Rishikesh, a global centre for yoga. This strategy worked. I also hosted a large number of journalists from abroad who began to write extensively about the state. An artists' camp was organised at Ananda, where, from two days of free hospitality, I managed to produce two dozen beautiful paintings of Uttarakhand in its different moods. Priceless. It is actually an unending list. India and the world finally woke up to a new tourism destination.

We also started improving the facilities at the famous sites and, at the same time, conceived major projects. Work was undertaken on a war footing to develop the ghats of the Ganga, the ski slopes at Auli, the airports at Jolly Grant and Pithoragarh, ropeways, signage, tourist information centres, the Char Dham or the Badrinath–Kedarnath–Yamnotri–

Gangotri pilgrimage routes, the lakes that dotted the state, the government-run tourist guesthouses, the iconic hill stations such as Mussoorie and Nainital, religious sites such as the Piran Kaliyar and Jageshwar temples, the trek route to the Kailash Mansarovar and so forth. Resources were always a major constraint, in the short run, in taking these projects to their logical conclusion, but over the years they have been successfully completed.

Keeping the lack of resources in mind, we started to look for private investment into major tourism projects. These included a top-class tourist resort at Tehri Dam, one of the highest water bodies in the world spanning twenty-eight square kilometres; a world-class ski resort at Dayara Bugyal in Uttarkashi, which experts cite as having the very best slopes; and an animal safari in the foothills of the Kumaon mountains. We also moved to lease the government-run tourist guesthouses to the private sector, a move which met with huge resistance from the vested interests who used them as their private property.

All the master plans were prepared with the best of technical expertise and input. However, I regret to say that I was unable to implement these ideas. Maybe I was being overambitious or just a little ahead of the times for the newly created state. It has remained a regret as well as a frustration. I do hope that someday these projects will come to fruition. The logic is simple—Uttarakhand must develop world-class infrastructure to attract foreign tourists. This, in turn, will have a huge impact on the economy of the state which largely relies on tourism as a source of income as well as employment. All the initiatives undertaken have been captured in a coffee-table book I authored—*A Road Well Taken*.

However, it is important to record my deep appreciation to successive chief ministers of Uttarakhand, Nityanand Swami, Bhagat Singh Koshiyari and NDT, who constantly backed and encouraged me. They stood with me against all my detractors who, at times, were my own cabinet ministers. Somehow, I have never understood why success arouses so much jealousy. Is it insecurity or simply envy? I have faced it throughout my career and Uttarakhand was no exception.

Another person who gave me complete and unequivocal support was the then Union minister for Tourism and Culture, Jagmohan. He was a man of tremendous vision and, during his numerous visits to the state, he guided me at every step. I had the privilege of travelling with him by road from Dehradun to Badrinath and over those two days, I picked up several ideas and concepts, not all restricted to tourism. I have always admired Jagmohan.

Our efforts in the area of tourism were paying off. Uttarakhand was being recognised. We were given a national award in 2003 for the best performing state amongst the newly created states and smaller states of India. But the crowning glory came in 2004 when, displacing states such as Kerala and Rajasthan, Uttarakhand received the golden elephant award for the best performing state in the field of tourism in India. This was a moment of huge joy and satisfaction for my team.

Information was my second area of focus. The journalists

were district-level and needed to think and grow in their thought processes with the formation of a state. I used my Kanpur experience to the hilt. First and foremost, I tried to win their trust by openly sharing information and constant dialogue. This is a must with journalists. One cannot go to them only when one needs them. However, one can approach them if a rapport and understanding is established. It has to be a relationship of mutual trust and confidence, not one based on suspicion. A lot of my colleagues treat journalists with suspicion and wariness. To my mind, this is a flawed approach. In any democratic set-up, the fourth estate is a critical pillar, and a good relationship with it is healthy for democracy. I did my best to establish this relationship with the press and media and I do not regret it one bit.

On the political front, Swami was replaced by Koshiyari as the chief minister a few months prior to the assembly elections in 2002. Koshiyari is the one who gave me the information portfolio. In February 2002, the Congress came to power in the state and, quite unexpectedly, NDT was deputed by Sonia Gandhi to head the state. Again, a quirk of fate. I was back with someone I had worked with in the chief minister's office in Uttar Pradesh. It was rumoured that I would be asked to serve as secretary in the office of NDT, now chief minister of Uttarakhand.

I met the chief secretary and conveyed my reluctance to do so on two counts. First, I was too involved in my work relating to tourism. Second, I did not want to be dubbed as NDT's 'man', a title very easily given to civil servants for no fault of theirs. I have always endeavoured to be a professional civil servant with absolutely no political leanings even though I have occupied key positions under the Congress, the Samajwadi Party as well as the BJP regimes. This has held me in good stead.

My assignment in Uttarakhand also provided me an opportunity to interact with several dignitaries such President A.P.J. Abdul Kalam, who visited the state to lay the foundation stone of the Uday Shankar Academy in Almora, then Prime Minister Dr Manmohan Singh, and then Home Minister Pranab Mukherjee who was the chairperson of the Nehru Institute of Mountaineering in Uttarkashi of which I was the secretary. I was closely associated with all of these visits.

From Dr Singh's visit, I remember two episodes. I accompanied NDT to receive the prime minister at the helipad. On embarking from the helicopter, Dr Singh folded his hands and remarked to NDT, 'Sir, you should not have come to the airport to receive me.' NDT smiled and we moved on. On the return, as NDT readied to see him off, I softly told him, 'Sir, the prime minister did not want you to go to the helipad.' NDT, in his inimitable style, held my hand and said, 'Prasad-ji, that is very gracious of Manmohan Singh-ji but let us not forget, today he is the prime minister and I am the chief minister. Propriety and protocol demand that I see him off.' It is a fact that NDT had been Dr Singh's boss at one time. This is called grace and dignity. The second was Dr Singh's remark after I had made a detailed presentation on our initiatives in the tourism sector. He smiled and said, 'This is truly world-class.'

I had three cabinet ministers to deal with, for information, sports and youth affairs, and tourism. It was always a tight ropewalk to balance the three and to give each of them the impression that they were equally important. I did not manage that to perfection. But NDT backed me fully and attempts by one of them to get rid of me bore no results. I survived with the same set of portfolios throughout my four-year stint in Uttarakhand. Another minister was the son of Gulab Singh, NDT's close confidant in the Uttar Pradesh days. My relationship with him remained professional and a bit distant. However, it would find a new branch several years later.

In April 2004, I received my orders for Central deputation to the same department where I had served as director during 1991–96, namely, the Department of Industrial Policy and Promotion. It was a rare occurrence to go back to the same place. I was a bit disappointed because I would have liked to serve in the Ministry of Tourism in Delhi. But, in a civil servant's career, things do not necessarily work out as planned. I requested the chief minister to relieve me and he refused point-blank. I had never seen NDT as angry before. He raised his voice and said, 'If all the good officers go to Delhi, what will happen to the state?' I waited in frustration but it was visible on my face. A few days later, after a late-night meeting with NDT and the chief secretary, the chief minister got up to leave, then stopped suddenly, came towards me, put his hand across my shoulder and gave his instructions to the chief secretary, 'Much as I regret to say so, please let him go and pursue his career in Delhi.' I was relieved the next day.

I left Uttarakhand feeling a sense of loss. I was going to miss Anjali's aunts, my loyal team and the working environment. Uttarakhand was a largely untouched state in terms of corruption, political machinations and petty jealousies. I had thoroughly enjoyed my stint in Uttarakhand and it gave me immense satisfaction to have made a small contribution in the growth and development of a newly created state.

Uttarakhand was the third state I had the privilege to work in; the other two being Tamil Nadu and Uttar Pradesh. I was one of the rare IAS officers who had the opportunity to work in three states of the country. I consider it my good luck to receive such a wide variety of experience and this explains my main motivation in penning down my experiences for future generations as well as those who would be interested in getting a peek into the lives of civil servants in India.

I left Dehradun with a teary farewell. The one who accompanied me to Delhi was my most faithful Bouncer.

CHAPTER ELEVEN

DELHI

The Sequel

I returned from Uttarakhand to a relatively empty house. Anjali was joint secretary in the Ministry of Agriculture and her job involved a fair amount of travel, mainly to Geneva, where she was a member of the Indian delegation to the Doha round of negotiations at the World Trade Organization (WTO). In March 2006, Anjali went back to Dehradun after completing her Central deputation. Urvashi was at the University of Cambridge in 2007. Overall, it was a disruptive phase in our family life. The only constant companion I had had since late 2005 was Bouncer.

I took charge as joint secretary, or a DG, in the Department of Industrial Policy and Promotion, on 25 April 2005. I had served in the same department at the level of deputy secretary/director during 1991–96. As such, I was familiar with the physical environment. I had an office in Udyog Bhawan, a much larger one than I had during my previous stint. A few other perks—like an official car—came with the job and a bigger team. The joint secretary function in the Government of India is important. They initiate policy documents and sign most of the proposals for consideration by the Union cabinet.

I met the secretary, whom I knew well. He had been instrumental in getting me on board in the department. I was told that the file concerning my work distribution was with the Minister of Commerce and Industry, Kamal Nath. Late one evening, I was invited to my first meeting with him. After the usual exchange of pleasantries, he announced my work allocation, saying I should look after the desk which handles intellectual property rights (IPRs).

My reaction, that can best be described as acute disappointment, was visible. He smiled and told me, 'This is the subject of the future' and went on to add, 'Please think big, have a forward-looking vision but make sure that the government is not embarrassed.' At the time, it was a Congress-led minority government backed by the left-wing parties. The ideological divide over IPRs in India at that stage was pretty stark. The left-wing parties viewed IPRs as a tool used by capitalists to exploit the masses. Others understood and appreciated the value that IPRs brought in incentivising innovation and technology development. Yet again, I found myself walking a tightrope.

Disappointment with my work allocation stemmed from various factors. First, it was my unfamiliarity with the subject matter. It was a sensitive and polarising issue. Also, it was not considered as glamorous an area as, say, foreign direct investment. After a couple of days, I decided to set aside my disappointment and submerge myself fully into this unknown space. As the months and years passed and my familiarity with IPRs grew, I became more and more fascinated. I became passionate about IPRs and began to love my work. I have Nath's foresight to thank for this.

The first challenge was to deal with the legal framework. The Indian Patent Act had to become TRIPS (Trade Related Intellectual Property Rights)-compatible. While the major amendments had been concluded before the deadline of 31 December 2004, through an ordinance, and the Patent Act amended prior to my joining, I had to deal with issues pertaining to the 'patentability' criteria and all the administrative work entailed in putting the new law into force. It was a pretty challenging task given that I was still trying to understand the basics of intellectual property law. In the end, I realised that the best way to acquire knowledge, even the legal framework, is through its practical implementation.

My next priority was to modernise the intellectual property infrastructure in India. It covered every aspect, from the physical to the digital, such as IP processes and products. In a record fifteen months, state-of-the-art infrastructure was created in the four metros of Delhi, Kolkata, Chennai and Mumbai as well as Ahmedabad. It would surprise many today that all the IP offices were previously located in private accommodation, which were so shabby that foreign guests who wanted to visit were often told they were closed on account of a local holiday. Modernisation did not stop at the physical infrastructure but included massive computerisation, introduction of e-filing, transparency measures, adherence to specified time limits and bolstering and training of human resources, to mention a few.

In the implementation of these modernisation plans, a major drawback was the lack of administrative experience at the level of the controller-general, who was someone from the cadre of the patent and trademark staff. I insisted that this position should go to an IAS officer and after a great deal of resistance, I finally succeeded. In retrospect, this has proved to be a pivotal step in the modernisation and development of the IP system in India.

A parliamentary committee headed by veteran BJP leader Murli Manohar Joshi (MMJ) in its first meeting was extremely critical of the IP infrastructure in the country. MMJ spoke about offices with cobwebs and was derisive of my explanations that the ground realities were now different. Soon after, I received a terse note from the parliament secretariat informing me that the entire parliamentary committee of twenty-five MPs would be visiting all the IP offices in the country. It also requested to organise meetings with the IP stakeholders at each venue. Handling the visit of a parliamentary committee is a major task but we managed well and everything went off smoothly. At the end of the visit, MMJ was gracious enough to concede that he was impressed with the work that had been done and his views had changed dramatically. We heaved a sigh of relief.

Next in our strategy was to learn from the experience of others. We, therefore, signed MOUs with the lead IP offices in the world, namely, the US, UK, France, Australia, Singapore, Japan, the Republic of Korea and the European Patent Office, to name a few. The MOUs explicitly stated that they would not cover either law or policy, which fell within the sole domain of Parliament and the Government of India. The MOUs covered capacity-building, training, modernisation and exchange programmes. Several of our staff went for short-term training to these IP offices. On their return, they apprised their colleagues of the global best practices. India's journey to being a robust, modern and forward-looking IP regime had started in these years and gathered steam a decade later.

In recognition of these efforts, a leading IP magazine, *Managing IP*, included me in its list of the fifty most influential persons in the world in this industry. It might have been a bit overstated but I must confess that it gave me a lot of personal satisfaction and joy.

My job also consisted of finding innovative solutions to practical problems. One such case dates back to 2006, when India was hit by bird flu. There was only one multinational pharmaceutical company in India which had a patent for the lifesaving drug, Tamiflu. The Ministry of Health demanded a supply of one million doses of Tamiflu. It recommended that the Ministry of Industry, being in-charge of the Patent Act, should apply compulsory licensing. It was an easy way out but I felt we should first find an alternative solution. There was no doubt in my mind that life must always take priority over all else, including IPRs. I convened a meeting with the multinational company that had invented Tamiflu and two major Indian pharmaceutical firms capable of producing generic versions of the drug. I first asked the patent holder whether they would be able to supply one million doses within ten days. The answer was 'no'. The maximum quantity they could commit to was 2,00,000. I gave them a clear choice. Either we would go in for compulsory licensing or they should enter into a royalty arrangement with the generic companies to provide the shortfall. It worked out smoothly.

The Ministry of Health had one million doses of Tamiflu in ten days and India avoided compulsory licensing. It was a win-win situation. This shows what innovative and creative thinking can do. This example may prove to be an extremely useful way forward in the near future given the COVID-19 pandemic. As and when a definitive treatment or vaccine is discovered, the principle of the 3As—accessibility, availability and affordability—will become of paramount importance. The world awaits with bated breath and, ironically, several stakeholders who have vigorously opposed compulsory licensing in the past are becoming its staunch proponents. The principle of life above all else is now being endorsed globally.

Throughout my tenure, I strongly advocated geographical indications (GIs) as a means of protecting India's rich and diverse cultural heritage. I was of the firm conviction that the protection of food and agricultural products would be beneficial to millions of Indian farmers. Starting with the famous Darjeeling tea to mangoes, handicrafts and centuries-old products made in remote villages of India, we advocated the grant of GIs. There were over 200 GIs. Several workshops were organised for stakeholders to understand the direct correlation between registering GIs, protecting their products and the economic benefits that accrued from doing so.

A great example was the GI registered for the famous Chanderi fabric, primarily saris. Chanderi fabric was manufactured in a township by that name located in the state of Madhya Pradesh, within the boundaries of the parliamentary constituency of Jyotiraditya Scindia, then a junior minister in the Dr Singh-led Congress government. Scindia was quick to grasp the importance of a GI for the Chanderi fabric. Next, he took steps to provide power looms and an adequate supply of water to the weavers located in Chanderi. A dying cottage industry began to boom once again and the GI gave protection from fake and counterfeit Chanderi products which had become the order of the day. A great example of putting IP to good economic use and for the benefit of people and their development.

A major area of focus for me was trademarks and designs. I initiated a cabinet note in February 2007 to commence the process of India's accession to the Madrid Protocol, a global system for the registration of trademarks and administered by WIPO. It took seven years for this process to fructify given the severe opposition from vested interests, primarily the legal community, who saw it as a blow on their monopolistic control over the registration of Indian trademarks abroad.

In the area of design, the possibilities of development and

growth are immense but still remain largely untapped. The National Institute of Design (NID), located in Ahmedabad, is a world-class institution. Strenuous efforts were made to strengthen this institution and expand its scope and reach. The first steps towards establishing four new NIDs in the country were initiated. A design council, led by a private sector representative, was also set up to advise the government on how to capitalise on the 'design' potential of the country. The mantra was: 'Success is not by chance; success is by design.'

In 2006, the Department of Industrial Policy and Promotion (DIPP) was designated as the nodal department for WIPO. It used to be called the Ministry of Human Resources until then. This entailed a great deal of additional work. WIPO was headed by Kamil Idris, a national of Sudan, and, at the insistence of the member states, was overseeing the hectic negotiations that entailed evolving a 'development agenda' for WIPO. I was deputed for most of the negotiations that were being held in Geneva. There seemed to be a complete deadlock between the developed and developing countries on various aspects of the development agenda. As the positions became more rigid, I sensed a breakthrough was elusive in the famous Room 'A' of WIPO, where most negotiations floundered. I offered to host a meeting offsite in Delhi as I was becoming increasingly convinced that only a change of scene may offer a way forward. This meeting, held in February 2007, was attended by twenty-two countries apart from the WIPO secretariat. Three days of hectic discussions and negotiations resulted in the impossible: an agreement. The WIPO secretariat was quick to capitalise on this situation and the next formal meeting saw the adoption of the development agenda for WIPO.

The next challenge was to create a body to oversee the work emanating from the development agenda projects. Several suggestions cropped up at the informal consultations led by Trevor Clarke, the permanent representative of Barbados to the United Nations in Geneva. These included a working group, a standing committee and an expert group. It was 2 a.m. and we were still closeted in informals in the Uchtenhagen meeting room, which was overflowing with delegates. No one seemed to back down from their positions. I was representing India along with a colleague, Radhey Shyam Julaniya. Like a bolt from the blue, I had an idea. What about naming it the 'Committee for Development and Intellectual Property'? I tentatively enquired of Radhey Shyam. 'Go ahead, Sir,' he said. I raised my hand. Trevor Clarke gave me a dismissive look but asked me to speak. I said, 'What about the Committee for Development and IP?' There was pin-drop silence and after thirty-odd seconds, Trevor Clarke gavelled the decision. It was the 'cut and thrust' training given to me by my additional secretary in negotiations at UNIDO that had paid off. I was thrilled at having contributed to a multilateral process in such a definitive manner.

Back in Delhi, IPRs was not my only charge. I was saddled with a host of disparate areas such as industrial sectors ranging from paper, cement and light engineering goods, to the Integrated Infrastructure Upgradation Scheme, the industrial policy for the north-eastern states as well as the establishment, general administration and vigilance sections for the entire ministry. I also handled work related to UNIDO as well as the Asian Productivity Organization. We were just two joint secretaries in those days. Today, this work is handled by five. As usual, I was overburdened, keeping nine-to-ten-hour schedules and working most weekends.

On one occasion, my responsibility for the general administration department created a very embarrassing situation for me. Two ministers of state were appointed in the ministry, one for industry and the other for commerce. I had the responsibility for locating a suitable office for the Minister of State (MoS) for Industry. The allocation of rooms for ministers was done by the estates department of the Ministry of Urban Development. I followed the drill and secured an allocation for the only room available in Udyog Bhawan. My colleagues in the Department of Commerce, instead of following this well-established protocol, simply broke the lock of the room allocated to the MoS, Industry, and settled their minister. The MoS, Industry, arrived the next morning to take charge. I welcomed him at the entrance to the Udyog Bhawan building and told him about what had transpired. I was clearly nervous. He was not. Coming from a legal background, he simply asked me, 'Are you on the right side of the law?' To my affirmative response, he smiled and breezed into 'his' office where the MoS, Commerce, was holding a meeting. With complete nonchalance, he greeted his colleague, went on to place a few idols on the sideboard and moved towards the main chair. I held my breath. I had never witnessed anything like this. Then with one wave of his hand he said, 'The hour designated as auspicious has arrived and I would like to take charge.' The MoS, Commerce, hesitated for a moment, gathered his papers, gave me a piercing look and left. What a smooth transition, I thought. A few days later, the MoS, Commerce, summoned me. I was prepared for a verbal firing. To my surprise he said, 'Look, I have ascertained the facts. My officers had not done their due diligence and were on the wrong side of the rules. You were right in what you did and I appreciate it.' By then the MoS, Commerce, had found a new office, displacing a senior officer in the ministry.

In March 2008, the coordination committee, an eighty-three-member body of WIPO, was to meet to elect a new DG. There were nearly a dozen candidates in the fray but the front-runners were Pakistan, Brazil and Australia. My mandate was to vote for Brazil; it was a developing country and also part of the Brazil, Russia, India, China and South Africa (BRICS) alignment. A small window was left open that in the ultimate race, India should back the winning horse. The delegation to the coordination committee comprised the ambassador, the deputy ambassador and myself. The voting went through several rounds and, as per the mandate, I voted consistently for Brazil. In the penultimate round, the Australian candidate, Gurry, led over Brazil's Jose Graca Aranha. I was approached by several developed countries to change India's vote. The ambassador also nudged me in that direction but sensing a close call, I did not wish to deviate from the mandate given to me. My vote in the last round also went to Brazil. It was a knife-edge contest with the Australian securing forty-two votes against forty-one by the Brazilian. The Indian delegation congratulated Gurry and, while there were several claimants to that one crucial vote, I told him quietly that even though we did not vote for him, we wished him success. I went back to the mission and filed a detailed report to Delhi. That report held me in good stead later on when some completely baseless rumours were spread stating that I had deviated from the mandate given to me. Also, what put the lid on this mudslinging was a categorical statement by my colleague, the deputy permanent representative.

Ten days later, on 23 May 2008, I received a call from Gurry, offering me the position as his chief of staff. I was taken aback. Here was someone for whom we had not voted offering me the most sensitive position in his administration. It was a direct offer. It took close to a year to get the necessary approvals in which my secretary in the department, Ajai Shankar, and the cabinet secretary played a key role. I relinquished my charge in the first week of May 2009 to take up my appointment as the chief of staff in WIPO.

This was sheer quirk of fate. In 2006, at the initiation of the sports secretary, Madhukar Gupta, the cabinet secretary requested for my lateral shift to the position of joint secretary, sports, in-charge of the Commonwealth Games, slated for 2010 in New Delhi. I was told the considerations were for an officer with a sports, industry and tourism background and who would be a go-getter. Flattered by these credentials, I was really excited about accepting this assignment. It would also give me a couple of years more on Central deputation at Delhi. The one who opposed it tooth and nail was Anjali. She intuitively felt it was a risky proposition.

In August 2006, I had lost one of my dearest persons, my mother, and was on leave recovering from her loss. On one of those days, I received a call from my secretary to see him for a very brief discussion. Very reluctantly, I went to his office. He showed me the proposal from the cabinet secretary recommending my transfer to the Ministry of Sports. I was in no mental state to apply my mind so I simply told him to go ahead. In a flash, he asked one of his assistants to take the file to the Minister of Commerce and Industry, Kamal Nath. He asked me to wait as he expected the file to be back in minutes. But the file did come back. There was a long noting on the file. I was mistaken. Anjali was not the only one opposed to my lateral shift. Nath was too. The rest is history.

CHAPTER TWELVE

WORLD INTELLECTUAL PROPERTY ORGANIZATION

WIPO, 2009 to 2020: Setting the Scene

My eleven-year stint at WIPO from 2009 to 2020 was a momentous one. This period saw a major shift in the global power structure. It began with the financial crisis in 2009 and ended with the COVID-19 pandemic, with huge implications for the global economy. A process of de-globalisation was set in motion. A new trend of placing nation states ahead of global alliances became the order of the day. A handful of very strong leaders with inward-looking policies sprang up in major countries across the globe. An immediate consequence of these tectonic shifts was the weakening of multilateral institutions, in particular, the UN system. Quite obviously, WIPO was also faced with these realities and needed to adjust to the rapidly evolving situation.

As a specialised agency of the UN, WIPO was tasked with the responsibility of protecting and promoting IPRs. These included patents, trademarks, designs and copyrights. The global IP landscape was pretty skewed, with the US and the developed world owning approximately eighty per cent of global IPRs. In turn, these countries had a major say in policies, strategies and—it would be no exaggeration to say—even in the day-to-day running of the organisation. This situation was further augmented by the fact that ninety-five per cent of WIPO's revenues came from fee for the services it rendered to IP rights holders. Clearly, the role of the developing world was very limited. However, the period from 2009 to 2020 saw a shift in the power balance, with China and some other developing countries such as Brazil, India, Russia, Republic of Korea and South Africa, to name a few, asserting themselves in a more forceful manner.

However, China was a clear leader. By 2020, China had emerged as the single largest filer of IP applications in WIPO, outstripping the US which had held this pivotal position since the organisation's inception. By the same time, Asia had displaced the US and Western Europe as the largest filer of IP applications in WIPO. These were incredible developments.

It was against this background that I took over as the chief of staff. My boss, the director general, Gurry, an Australian, was viewed as a votary of the developed world. There was a clear trust deficit between the DG and the developing world. On the one hand, I knew that I had to move in consonance with the evolving situation globally; on the other, I had to deal with the widely held perception that Gurry was first and foremost a promoter of the interests of the developed world and little else. It was going to be a tightrope walk.

Gurry's election to the post of the DG in 2008 had been a highly polarised one. This was to cast its shadow on his entire first term. In fact, politics overtook all else even in the months leading up to Gurry's confirmation as DG by the general assemblies of WIPO and his assumption of office. Efforts were made to reopen the election process, spread a scurrilous campaign against Gurry and to leave no stone unturned to make his entry into the office a difficult one. A seed of bitterness, falsehood and vindictiveness was sown with dire consequences for the organisation. Some individuals, who would later assume important positions in the administration, made the most of the situation. They played on Gurry's insecurities, lit bushfires and thereafter doused them to earn his attention and favour in the years to come.

Gurry took charge as planned on 1 October 2008. He was a WIPO insider, having joined the organisation in 1985 and risen to the rank of deputy director general (DDG) in 2003. As such he was fully conversant with the organisation. He knew almost all the staff by name. It was both an advantage as well as a handicap. Handicap in the sense that he held very firm views on most of the staff, some not very objective or fair. I would have to guard against being saddled with this baggage.

Gurry was a world-renowned authority on IPRs and a man of great intellect. He was also a man in a hurry. He wanted to reform and structurally redefine the organisation at supersonic speed. The intensity was felt by most but nowhere more than the DG's office. To say the least, it was going to be a challenging task for me.

WIPO: 2009

I joined WIPO as chef de cabinet, later titled as chief of staff, on 11 May 2009. Geneva is known for its magnificent hotels, palaces that line the lakefront with amazing views and top-class service. I thought that a couple of weeks in such accommodation—pending finding an apartment—would alleviate the burden of separation from my family in India when I first arrived. The first weeks away from home are so difficult. Unfortunately, that is not how things played out.

A few days after receiving word that I had won the competition for the post of chief of staff and confirming my acceptance, I received a phone call from a soft-spoken lady saying that she was from WIPO, asking if I needed help finding accommodation in Geneva. I was thrilled. My apprehensions about the organisation—formed as a delegate covering WIPO for many years—were fading. Such a warm reception! She asked me if I had any preferences for location. I said anywhere in town, lakeside would be perfect. At this point, she said there were no options in Geneva. The apprehensions were coming back. It reminded of some flights I had taken and the stuffy airline hostess would come by with the meal tray and ask: 'Meat or chicken?' I would say 'chicken' to which the hostess would respond, 'There is no more chicken.' So why in the world are you giving me the option? Why was this lady giving me an option when none existed? So, I ended up in a dump in neighbouring France. I later found out there were hotel options in Geneva. Till this day, I suspect the colleague owned shares in the hotel in neighbouring France given that she kept putting up new arrivals there.

My first day in Geneva started with a bus journey from Ferney to the Palais, in front of the imposing WIPO building, one of the most iconic office spaces in Geneva, built in 1978, but pretty ageless in appearance. I was received at the reception and escorted to the famous eleventh floor which housed the DG's office. It reminded me of the fifth floor of the Lucknow Secretariat Annexe where I spent three years in the CMO. This assignment was going to be for only two years, I told myself. I could not have been farther from the reality!

The eleventh floor presented a fairly confused picture. Later I was to realise that in the six months prior to my taking charge, several decisions were taken which would have a deleterious effect on the organisation. This was not the DG's fault. He was surrounded by a bunch of highly ambitious staff who were adept at wielding power but totally lacked administrative experience and maturity. The cabinet consisted of colleagues who worked in silos and thought they were the last word on whatever they handled. What made matters worse was the lack of administrative and managerial acumen in the office of the director general.

My office was at one end of the corridor; at the other end was the DG's office. There was a flurry of activity; a desktop computer was being set up. My deputy, who occupied this room, was collecting his papers, the DG was not in the office and most colleagues on the floor gave me searching and, if I may say, unfriendly looks. I felt I had somehow rocked the boat and the questions uppermost in the minds of colleagues was: who is he and what is his style of functioning going to be. Not to be cowed down with this rather unfriendly reception, I decided to meet each one of the colleagues individually. It was quite an experience. Right from getting coached on WIPO's finances to being blocked from entering some offices, I had a taste of the most unusual reception. Then came my letter of appointment which I was expected to sign. It showed my contract for four years instead of two, which was my understanding. I pointed this out to the rather officious-looking human resource representative and got a terse response, 'These are the instructions of the DG.'

Next, I met the DG. He clearly spelled out my initial tasks. To set the DG's office in order, to serve as the secretary to the governing bodies of WIPO, and to assist in the DG's negotiations with member states on the selection of the new senior management team. It was a handful and on the very first day itself I was thrown into what would define my job at WIPO over the next decade.

The first task was to streamline the procedures for files and papers in the DG's office. There was complete lack of systems. Coming from a well-established bureaucracy like India, putting basic systems for the movement of files and papers was a relatively easy task. Next, I tried to create a team and break the silos between colleagues by a daily meeting where we reviewed the incoming mail, the appointments and visits of the DG and all issues where we were expected to assist him. We decided to be a nameless, faceless cabinet working from behind the scenes rather than one which was visible and out there. This proved to be a perfect model in the long run.

As secretary to the governing bodies, I had a mammoth task. It entailed both logistical as well as substantive issues and involved our key stakeholders, the member states. The DG had the vision to create a separate division called the Assemblies Affairs and Documentation Division. The organisation of WIPO meetings, as I had observed as a delegate, were, to say the least, disorganised and shabby. Documents were often handed over to delegates after the agenda item had been introduced, seating arrangements were free for all, there was no time limit for delivery of statements with the agenda item on 'opening statements' taking more than two days to be completed, the only social event was a reception on day one, member state engagement was low. The list can go on. It was quite a task to convert this situation into what we see today.

WIPO meetings are now organised and conducted in a flawless manner, replete with member state cultural and social events and often cited as a role model for the UN system. It has been an honour for me to serve as secretary to the governing bodies for the past eleven years. In this capacity, I have served more than 250 WIPO assemblies and other WIPO committees and unions. It has been a very enriching experience to say the least.

In the context of organising the assemblies, I feel compelled to state that our role was not limited to simply ensuring perfect logistics. It went beyond that. One of the chairs of the general assemblies was a rather impatient man. He also wanted to conduct the assemblies with precision and in a clockwork manner. In keeping with this, he insisted that speakers, two at a time, be seated on the podium in advance of their speaking slots. Bearing this in mind, I asked a colleague to politely escort the next speaker, who happened to be a minister, to the podium. A couple of minutes elapsed but there was no sign of either the minister or my colleague. The chair nudged me a couple of times, inquiring about the next speaker. I told him we were on the job. Meanwhile, the speaking slot came and the chair decided to skip the minister and go on to the next speaker. The chair was fuming and directed his wrath towards me. In turn, I was livid with the 'inefficiency' of my colleague. At that juncture, my colleague clambered on to the podium and, after hearing a mouthful from me, asked for a moment to explain. It seems the minister was fast asleep when my colleague approached him. A gentle tap on the shoulder woke him up. Next it seems he had lost his shoes, which my colleague had to retrieve and place at the minister's feet. That done, the minister wished to visit the 'men's' and wanted my colleague to accompany him. All this took a good ten minutes. The minister lost his speaking slot, my colleague almost lost his job for his inefficiency and I was accused by the chair for not facilitating a smooth flow of the proceedings. These are the travails of the multilateral world behind all the glitz and glamour associated with it.

My work as secretary brought me into close touch with senior member state representatives, mostly ambassadors who served as chairs of the various assemblies and bodies. They came from different corners of the world with very different experiences and even more diverse perceptions. My interactions with the numerous chairs were interesting, revealing, frustrating as well as a real test of my patience at times. I could not have hoped for a better space to understand first-hand the complex maze of the world of multilateral diplomacy.

When I first arrived in Geneva, I thought it would be a good idea to visit a number of missions to introduce myself to ambassadors. Some were uneventful. I arrived, was well received, presented myself, talked about my vision for building a constructive dialogue, exchanged niceties and returned to my eleventh-floor office. But not all meetings were smooth. One of the first calls I made was on the permanent representative and ambassador of India to the United Nations in Geneva and I received a decidedly frosty reception. I began to wonder why the world seems pitted against me. There is no other explanation except petty jealousies and envy, something which is not in our control. The same ambassador did everything under the sun to make my stay in Geneva a difficult one. He simply wanted me to leave. Canards were spread about me. The Indian delegation took unusual positions in WIPO. Official statements, couched in diplomatic language, were made against me. It was relentless but I decided to battle it out rather than succumb.

Another of my early diplomatic calls stood out for its eccentricity. I was accompanied by my deputy at the time—for better or for worse, a role that quickly ceased to exist—as we arrived at the entrance of a building that showed its age. I have always wondered how one of the most beautiful cities in the world could allow boring concrete buildings to sprout everywhere. For a city that is so strict that it penalises toilet flushers after 10 p.m., I couldn't understand the laxity with the architecture. I was told it was part of a trend in the 1970s but that no one can really explain or justify.

Just as inexplicable was the bizarre reception that we received upon arrival. As we entered the apartment that housed the mission, we were received by a kind, discreet receptionist lacking any curiosity or apparent passion for the job. I had already come across the phenomenon in my first days in Geneva, so I wasn't particularly fazed by the attitude. After a few minutes, we were escorted into the ambassador's office. He sat perched on what was more throne than chair, behind a huge desk that was clearly two sizes too big for the space. He stayed seated. I thought that was a bit odd. Perhaps my expectations were too high, perhaps it was part of the cultural diversity that characterises the international organisations scene. Whatever the reason, that was the bland welcome that my deputy and I received.

The kind lady pointed to the couch in the corner of the office and left. I think it was at that moment that I decided to put an end to my initiative to call on ambassadors. Time seemed to stop. I was trapped. Do I reciprocate the lack of diplomacy that I was confronted by? Or do I wait it out to its natural end and find humour in the absurdity of the moment. And just then, my thoughts were interrupted by a humming noise. Was it a dysfunctional AC machine? A kettle of boiling water? No. It was coming from the throne. The ambassador still hadn't said a word. He hummed. Incidentally, that was after he served himself a glass of orange juice. Emphasis on 'himself'.

The wait seemed endless. The normality of my eleventh-floor office seemed so far away. And then, the ambassador decided to speak. 'Mary,' he called. The kind lady who received us appeared in the office. The ambassador then summoned Mary to 'do it'. At this point I was praying for a superpower to allow me to just disappear! What was Mary being asked to do? Mary was feeling very uncomfortable and pleaded with the ambassador to let her return to her desk. But he insisted. And Mary obliged. She began to recite a prayer. A couple of minutes later and the sign of the Trinity completed, the ambassador finally turned to us and said, 'Hello, Mr Prasad, it's nice to meet you.'

The ambassador went on to explain, 'I had to get this meeting blessed as I have had a terrible experience with WIPO.' I couldn't help but enquire why. He said that he had requested WIPO's annual report on three occasions and had not received even one yet. My patience was clearly wearing thin and I decided to put him out of his misery regarding the mysterious missing annual reports. 'Ambassador,' I said, 'WIPO doesn't publish annual reports.' He shot back a cold, confused glare from atop the throne. This time, I reciprocated with an equally cold thank you and goodbye. That was my first brush with the complexities (and eccentricities) of Geneva's multilateral diplomacy.

I also served as the Sherpa to the DG who was a member of the chief executives board headed by the secretary general of the United Nations. It had as members all heads of UN agencies along with the president of the World Bank and the chief executive of the International Monetary Fund. I was only a passive participant at these meetings, but it was indeed a learning experience to follow the discussions at this key forum for the UN.

During 2009, I accompanied the DG on two high-profile visits: one to Singapore and the other to India. In Singapore, we met with the prime minister as well as several ministers. In the island nation, at the highest echelons of government, there was a high level of awareness regarding the utility of promoting and protecting IPRs, something which was fairly absent in India.

One particular engagement of our visit to Singapore truly impressed me. It was a visit to a kindergarten school where some tiny tots performed a play. The theme of the play was piracy and counterfeiting, and the message was simple, loud and clear: piracy and counterfeiting were tantamount to theft. It was telling that a message on piracy and counterfeiting was being transmitted and instilled in the minds of very young kids. It was part of the education process. An effort was being made to inculcate a respect for IPRs and ingrain it in the value system—something which should be done in the Indian education system as well, I thought. That way we could prevent Palika Bazaar-like markets flourishing in India selling counterfeit and pirated goods. Indeed, the play by kids in Singapore left a lasting impression on me.

The visit to New Delhi in November 2009 was a truly impressive one. The DG called on the prime minister of India, Dr Singh, as well as seven of his cabinet colleagues. The meeting with Dr Singh was a fascinating one as in his well-known scholarly style he laid out the IP landscape in India, its strengths and weaknesses and the possible role that a multilateral agency such as WIPO could play in strengthening the ecosystem in India. As a parting remark, he looked at me and told the DG, 'You have stolen one of our brightest stars.' It was just the grace that as an Indian prime minister he wished to show a fellow Indian in the presence of a foreign dignitary who happened to be my boss. I will forever be indebted to Dr Singh for this very charitable comment, something which is getting more and more rare these days. The solidarity that we should be showing our fellow Indians, especially abroad, is fast eroding as a cultural ethos. While this may sound as a sweeping generalisation, this conclusion is based on my own experience.

On 1 December 2009, the new members of the senior management team took charge. It comprised the DG, four deputy directors general, three assistant directors general and myself. The induction of the senior management team was conducted at a resort just outside Geneva in neighbouring France. The DG gave a detailed briefing about his priorities over the next five years followed by a very absorbing brainstorming session. There was a lot of bonhomie, and the evening drinks and dinner turned out to be an evening to remember. It augured well, I thought. The future had another story to tell!

The year 2009 ended on a very satisfactory note. I had reorganised the DG's office, held reasonably successful general assemblies, built an excellent rapport with my boss, was receiving a lot of appreciation from one and all, in particular the DG, but this was all going to change very soon. Success has many enemies and I would be the victim of my own.

WIPO: 2010

As I was settling down and my work was being publicly acknowledged by the DG, there were forces that began to work against me. This opposition came from the Indian mission, insiders within WIPO and by one particular individual who had always eyed my position. Every effort was made to create a misunderstanding between the DG and myself and after a fantastic first year, our relationship became cold and distant. The honeymoon was getting over faster than expected, almost proving my detractors, who had predicted my survival in this position to no more than six months. Gurry, in any case, did not have a great reputation for lasting relationships. He was famous for his quick shift from a colleague being 'outstanding' to just being 'OK' before finally declaring the staff member as an 'outright disaster' or someone as being 'high maintenance'.

I had the challenge of stemming the usual slide in his perceptions!

Tensions were stirred up in January 2010 over an innocuous mail that I had sent requesting the vice-chair from Egypt to hold an informal meeting of the Program and Budget Committee, as the chair of the committee, a French diplomat, had moved out of Geneva. This mail was sent at the request of the controller, a French national. But an impression was created that I was favouring the Egyptian over the French, which was blatantly false. However, given the acute insecurity that existed at that time between the developed and the developing world, it was very easy for my detractors to spin this yarn. Unfortunately, the DG fell for this bizarre logic and confronted me. As my conscience was totally clear, I refuted the allegation strongly. The air was temporarily cleared. But this was only the beginning of a campaign to bring a divide between the DG and me.

In April 2010, the DG received an anonymous complaint against me, alleging that I was trying to be an aspirant to his position. Someone who knew the DG very well was feeding his insecurities. It was a most incredible allegation. The DG's term had just begun and he had another five years to go. How could anybody possibly be an aspirant to his position? I decided to get the anonymous piece of paper, received through a fax machine, investigated. It showed a number which the Geneva Police told me was from a drug peddler from Somalia who was an undertrial in several acts of criminality. Why on Earth would this drug peddler write an anonymous complaint against me? It was obviously at the behest of someone else. If I wished to pursue the case, I would need to appear in the local courts and it would have made big news so I decided not to press the matter. In retrospect, I wish I had because I could only close the loop in the matter several years later. An unknown enemy was at work!

In June 2010, following a meeting of the senior management team, I sent a long communication to the DG setting the 'Lakshman rekha' for our relationship. This was a direct reaction to what had transpired at that meeting. The communication spelt out that I would never accept being publicly snubbed or humiliated, that I had heard several rumours that someone from the Australian mission was to replace me and that I did not wish to keep the seat warm and, finally, that I would never accept a disparaging comment about my country. I did not receive an acknowledgement.

In July 2010, while on a visit to Bangladesh, sitting in the lobby of the Taj Hotel, the DG suddenly told me in a sharp and nervous tone that he intended to appoint a strategic adviser (SA). The impression he conveyed was that I would oppose this move. I simply shrugged my shoulder. The rest of the visit, which otherwise was very successful, including a meeting with Prime Minister Sheikh Hasina, proved to be tense and challenging.

On the last day of our stay, a dinner was hosted by Bangladesh's foreign minister to which several ministers were invited. The DG had to leave early to catch his flight back to Geneva, so I took his place at the head table. A very interesting conversation ensued. One of the ministers waxed eloquent about Rabindranath Tagore belonging to Bangladesh. I chose to ignore it. What followed was a discussion on mangoes and then one of them went on to say that the best mangoes were from Bangladesh. Even before I could react, the Minister of Agriculture snapped back and said, 'We have to be balanced and reasonable and simply accept that the best mangoes come from India.' Once again, I did not need to say anything.

WIPO: 2011

In June 2011, an SA was appointed with a very unclear job description. She was a diplomat from the Australian mission. All kinds of rumours were afloat that she would ultimately replace me. The perception in the organisation was that she was very close to the DG and very soon most colleagues began to perceive her as the de facto head. In reality, nothing could be further from the truth. I broached the DG for a frank discussion. He assured me that my role and responsibilities would remain unchanged and that while I would look at 'internal' issues, she would deal with the diplomatic community and the staff council. This appointment proved to be a disaster for the DG.

The SA went well beyond her terms of reference. The relationship between the DG and the SA became tense and frosty. In March 2012, the SA blew the whistle on what was considered as transfer of sensitive IT equipment to Iran and North Korea. A communication was sent out to all member states. An unprecedented breach of procedures. In the end, Gurry was absolved of all the charges in this respect but it brought him into the eye of an avoidable storm and one which was deeply resented by the US and other developed countries. In the aftermath of this development, the SA resigned by the end of 2012 but her action left a deep scar on Gurry's first tenure as DG. It also sowed the seed of what was to become a bitter and malicious campaign against him in the years to come, almost jeopardising his second term.

The SA had gone well beyond her remit in other matters as well. She interfered in almost all departments of the organisation and created the impression that her assessment would determine whether the Australian government would give a nomination to the DG for a second term. Most people bought this claim hook, line and sinker, but coming from a seasoned bureaucracy like India, I did not give any credence to such claims. It was amazing to see how naive most of my colleagues could be in believing some of the SA's most incredible claims. I had good reasons not to believe her because just before she joined WIPO, she asked me to a lunch. The conversation at that meal was one-sided. It was the future SA carrying out a tirade against the DG, making him out to be a tyrant, a bully yet emotionally a very weak person. I was tongue-tied. Here was someone who owed her high-level appointment to the DG running him down ruthlessly. She even tore into the DG's family. I couldn't believe my ears. The level of disloyalty was shocking to say the least. I was in a dilemma. Should I tell the DG about this conversation? But, unfortunately, trust levels between us had gone so low that I felt he might think I was simply insecure and wanted to block her entry into the organisation. The Dhaka conversation and my reaction to it came back. I simply decided to 'shrug' but took a firm resolve that I would never trust this person. Nor would I let her interfere in my work. I would continue to work professionally and loyally. This is our training as Indian civil servants and I would not allow a dent in that at any cost.

WIPO, 2014 to 2020

The year 2014 was significant. Gurry faced huge opposition from his own DDG, who was from the United States. In violation of established norms, a public complaint was made by the DDG against Gurry. Instead of resorting to the internal justice system, he chose to send his letter of complaint to all member states of WIPO. This was the beginning of a deliberate campaign to malign Gurry and stall his chances for a second term. However, the election results belied the machinations of his detractors and Gurry won a second term in a most convincing manner. The significant point was that his support base had shifted from developed to developing countries. Gurry was no longer seen as a votary of only the developed world but rather as a friend of the developing world. This was a huge change of perception and one that I would consider as a key element of Gurry's leadership at WIPO.

The complaint from the DDG went on to be investigated by the Office of Internal Oversight, the independent audit and oversight body of the UN. It became the subject of great discussion amongst member states but finally Gurry was cleared of all the charges in the autumn of 2016. It was a bizarre campaign against the head of a UN agency with all the trappings of intrigue, maliciousness and vendetta. What was most disconcerting was that several important member states, who had begun to feel alienated from Gurry, made the most of the situation to settle petty scores. Having a ringside view of the entire chain nauseated me. While I had seen all kinds of intrigues and conspiracies in India, to witness something as base and coarse such as this was shocking. To think that the UN is all about ethical conduct and fair play could not be further from the truth. In the end, Gurry came out unscathed. The campaign against him continued but was not successful enough and he had a most satisfying and productive four years before demitting charge, on completion of his tenure, on 30 September 2020. Gurry left the organisation in very good shape, a well-oiled machinery with a robust financial status. It would be no exaggeration to say that Gurry was the architect of a new WIPO, one that is strong, resilient and, above all, inclusive. In trying to make it an inclusive organisation he faced several hurdles and in fact paid a heavy personal price. However, he will go down in the annals of WIPO's history as a leader who was deeply committed to the organisation and its well-being. I, for one, stood to gain a lot from this experience in terms of getting an insight into international diplomacy and powerplay at the highest echelons of the UN system.

On 1 October 2020, Daren Tang, a national from Singapore,

took charge as the DG of WIPO. I was requested to continue for a period of three months to help with the transition. A new era was dawning. For the first time in WIPO's history, a rank outsider who had never worked in the organisation was taking charge. Clearly, the dynamics were going to be different. For the better or the worse, only time will tell.

My assignment at WIPO gave me an opportunity to travel to different parts of the world in different capacities. At times, I simply accompanied the DG. On other occasions, I represented the DG at important events. I also visited the WIPO external offices in Singapore, China and the Russian Federation. These travels and visits gave me great exposure to the world that lay beyond the staid and secure confines of WIPO headquarters in Geneva.

On the staff front, slowly but surely a great team built up in the cabinet, some of whom have spent more than a decade with me. It was a unique as well as fascinating experience to deal with colleagues from different parts of the world. Therein also lay the challenge. As I always say, the real test for a national civil servant is to seamlessly transit into an international civil servant. It's no easy task to shed the 'national mindset' and adjust to the 'international milieu'. Only some succeed; most flounder.

My relationship with Gurry was not without its ups and downs, particularly in the initial years. But, as we progressed, the relationship matured into one of trust and friendship. Gurry is a man of great intellect and drive. His commitment to WIPO was constant. He was a hard taskmaster and intolerant of anything less than perfect. He worked with a passion that I have rarely seen. He could be harsh and brusque, particularly with his pen, but it was always short-lived. He was compassionate with respect to personal matters. Extremely well read and with a masterly command over language, his sense of humour was amazing. I did have my share of difficult times with him but I was also very fortunate to be so closely associated with him. It was a great learning experience. I thoroughly enjoyed our lunch outings in the WIPO cafeteria and more than the food it was the wide array of topics that we discussed—from cricket to pets, from politics to philosophy. Gurry happened to be my boss for the longest period in my career.

My work portfolio continued to grow. From managing the affairs of the office of the DG to supervising the Assemblies Affairs and Documentation Division, I went on to oversee work related to protocol and event management, external offices, communications and business continuity.

External offices were a difficult wicket to bat on. It was a politically surcharged subject with member states polarised on the opening and functioning of new external offices and the role of the secretariat. Our efforts in this direction were duly recognised by the senior management team which recommended the external offices for a 'working as one' reward in 2020.

The protocol and event management division acquired a completely new dimension over the last five years. A pivotal decision to open the WIPO infrastructure for use by WIPO member states and stakeholders was a real game-changer. This decision had met with strong resistance from within the organisation by those who preferred the status quo; WIPO's infrastructure should remain for use by WIPO staff only. The DG decided to overrule this inward-looking minority. Today, WIPO is the preferred venue for a host of social and cultural events, adding a very rich veneer to an organisation which deals with a rather terse and legalistic subject such as IPRs. It has worked wonders in terms of soft diplomacy and the goodwill that we have received from our key stakeholders.

The communications division was totally restructured and split into three divisions so as to give the key areas such as news and social media, publications, and marketing and branding the focus they deserve. Three directors were appointed to head these divisions. However, it was made sure that they do not work in silos. Visible impact is now being felt and seen as a result of this restructuring process.

The area of business continuity came in for a severe test during the COVID-19 pandemic. Since WIPO depends on its services for ninety-five per cent of its revenues, it was imperative for business continuity to be maintained. It was a mammoth task to get the premises vacated, make 1,200 staff functional from home and ensure that our business needs were fulfilled. The health, safety and security of all staff was of paramount importance. A fine balance had to be struck. Assisted by the crisis response and the crisis communications teams, a foolproof and resilient strategy was worked out. It paid great dividends. We had a WIPO fully safe and secure for its staff as well as working at productivity levels beyond expectations. In recognition of the efforts of these incredible teams, the senior management team unanimously decided to constitute a special reward for the crisis response team. As the coordinator, I felt both honoured and humbled.

My eleven years in WIPO have been a most remarkable journey. It had its moments of highs and lows, ups and downs, but as I look back, these were truly exceptional years. I would be perhaps the longest-serving chief of staff in the UN system. That too in a very complex and difficult milieu. I learnt a lot, contributed in my own small way but it made me a wiser and richer human being. An invaluable experience to say the least.

On the personal front, Anjali joined me in Geneva in May 2014, to take over as India's permanent representative and ambassador to the WTO. It was a prestigious assignment and one for which she was fully equipped in terms of experience. We moved into a beautiful apartment on the lakefront, opposite the Jet d'Eau, where Urvashi and I had spent hours in 1994 while Anjali attended a course at the WTO. Not in our wildest dreams could we have imagined that one day we would live in one of the most beautiful and high-end apartments in the world, that too with such a glorious view! But more than anything else, it was simply great to be reunited with Anjali, my most precious and valued partner in my journey of life.

In 2010-11, Urvashi pursued her higher studies at the London School of Hygiene and Tropical Medicine. She had turned out to be a very accomplished girl. In 2016, Urvashi married Ambesh. The marriage was solemnised in Bhopal with a reception in Delhi. Several of my colleagues, including Gurry, attended the wedding. It was a week of festivities, fun and frolic, at the end of which we had added a son to our family. I had always thought it would be difficult for me to part with the apple of my eye but as they say, 'A daughter is a daughter all your life.' Nothing could be truer.

My fondest memories from my days in WIPO will be my association with several of my colleagues. Some have stood out for their hard work and some for their support. It was in Geneva that I discovered some of the best people in my life, friends and family put together. I gained enduring relationships, but in 2014 I lost one of my closest friends from my Kanpur days. In 2011, I had lost Bouncer, whom I considered more my friend than a mere pet. As they say, in the cycle of life you gain some, you lose some! And life goes on in its cyclical way. We are only small cogs in a large, revolving wheel which takes us up and down, high and low.

AFTERWORD

My father was an astute and highly skilled civil servant. He was one of the rare Indian Administrative Service (IAS) officers to serve in three very diverse states across the country. He handled many difficult situations during his career as an administrator, including those with challenging political, social and communal dimensions. And then with consummate ease, he transitioned from being an IAS officer to an international diplomat. The fact that he could unite a motley group of people in a United Nations body is a testament to his incredible leadership abilities. He transformed the organisation from a white man's club into one which was inclusive and served the interests of all nations and people.

At a personal level, he was the most dedicated husband and father who managed to strike a remarkable balance between his very demanding profession and family life. He would often narrate experiences from his life to his family and friends, and what always stood out was that he was an incredible, witty storyteller with a superlative sense of humour. What surprised all of us was that he typed this entire book on his mobile phone! He used the time spent at home after the COVID-19 pandemic hit the world to pen this incredible memoir, which offers rich insights into the journey of a civil servant and also many important lessons, without ever getting preachy—true to his characteristic style.

Urvashi Prasad

ABOUT THE AUTHOR

Naresh Nandan Prasad, an alumnus of St. Stephen's College, Delhi University, held a double master's degree in history and economics. Prasad's professional career spanned almost forty-five years, with about thirty-one years in the Indian Administrative Service (IAS, 1981 batch UP/Uttarakhand cadre) and over fourteen years in the United Nations—United Nations Industrial Development Organization (UNIDO) and World Intellectual Property Organization (WIPO).

In his long career in the IAS, Prasad gained administrative and technical experience at the national, state and local levels in the areas of rural and urban development, law and order management, conduct of elections, media management, industrial policy, tourism, intellectual property rights and multilateral negotiations. Besides having worked in the central government, Prasad was one of the rare IAS officers to have worked in three totally diverse states of India—Tamil Nadu, Uttar Pradesh and Uttarakhand.

As the Chief Development Officer in Aligarh for three years, he worked on all aspects of development—from health, sanitation and infrastructure to water, forestry, energy and education. During his tenure, Aligarh was awarded the best-performing district in Uttar Pradesh in renewable energy.

As the Chief Executive Officer of the Development Authority of Kanpur, Prasad floated the first-ever infrastructure bond issued by a body, which led to a re-organisation of its finances, based on an A+ credit rating from India's leading ratings agency.

Prasad served for about fifteen years in the field of industry and commerce and had extensive multilateral experience. He was India's focal point for UNIDO, WIPO and the Asian Productivity Organization. As part of India's economic liberalisation in the early 1990s, he organised the first Investment and Technology Market, attracting foreign direct investment to India. In 1995, he was responsible for organising the Global Forum on Industry, which dealt with, among other issues, industrial and technological partnerships. He played a key role in modernising the country's intellectual property infrastructure and was responsible for intellectual property negotiations at multilateral and bilateral levels. He facilitated India's accession to the Madrid Protocol on Trademarks and was responsible for formulating and implementing India's design policy.

Prasad featured in the list of the Top 10 most influential people in the Asia-Pacific, brought out in 2008 by the leading IP magazine, *Managing Intellectual Property*.

Naresh Nandan Prasad was assistant director general and chief of staff to the director general of WIPO and, as such, was among the senior-most Indians within the UN. In this capacity, he offered strategic advice to and managed the director general's office, acted as secretary to the WIPO General Assemblies and oversaw the work of WIPO's apex body as well as that of over 250 other governing bodies, coordinated WIPO's network of six external offices, managed WIPO's internal and external communications and protocol and events services.

During his tenure of over twelve years, Prasad contributed significantly towards turning WIPO into a well-managed, proactive and responsive organisation. However, one of his most important contributions was towards turning a hitherto 'white man's club', as WIPO was called, into an inclusive organisation accessible to all its members, big or small, rich or poor.

Prasad passed away in July 2021. He is survived by his wife, daughter and son-in-law.